The European VC-Funded Startup Guide

Create and Manage a Startup in Eastern Europe

Ivan Voras

Apress®

The European VC-Funded Startup Guide: Create and Manage a Startup in Eastern Europe

Ivan Voras
Zagreb, Croatia

ISBN-13 (pbk): 978-1-4842-9519-9 ISBN-13 (electronic): 978-1-4842-9520-5
https://doi.org/10.1007/978-1-4842-9520-5

Copyright © 2023 by Ivan Voras

This work is subject to copyright. All rights are reserved by the Publisher, whether the whole or part of the material is concerned, specifically the rights of translation, reprinting, reuse of illustrations, recitation, broadcasting, reproduction on microfilms or in any other physical way, and transmission or information storage and retrieval, electronic adaptation, computer software, or by similar or dissimilar methodology now known or hereafter developed.

Trademarked names, logos, and images may appear in this book. Rather than use a trademark symbol with every occurrence of a trademarked name, logo, or image we use the names, logos, and images only in an editorial fashion and to the benefit of the trademark owner, with no intention of infringement of the trademark.

The use in this publication of trade names, trademarks, service marks, and similar terms, even if they are not identified as such, is not to be taken as an expression of opinion as to whether or not they are subject to proprietary rights.

While the advice and information in this book are believed to be true and accurate at the date of publication, neither the authors nor the editors nor the publisher can accept any legal responsibility for any errors or omissions that may be made. The publisher makes no warranty, express or implied, with respect to the material contained herein.

>   Managing Director, Apress Media LLC: Welmoed Spahr
>   Acquisitions Editor: Shivangi Ramachandran
>   Development Editor: James Markham
>   Editorial Project Manager: Shaul Elson
>   Copy Editor: Mary Behr

Cover designed by eStudioCalamar

Distributed to the book trade worldwide by Springer Science+Business Media LLC, 1 New York Plaza, Suite 4600, New York, NY 10004. Phone 1-800-SPRINGER, fax (201) 348-4505, e-mail orders-ny@springer-sbm.com, or visit www.springeronline.com. Apress Media, LLC is a California LLC and the sole member (owner) is Springer Science + Business Media Finance Inc (SSBM Finance Inc). SSBM Finance Inc is a **Delaware** corporation.

For information on translations, please e-mail booktranslations@springernature.com; for reprint, paperback, or audio rights, please e-mail bookpermissions@springernature.com.

Apress titles may be purchased in bulk for academic, corporate, or promotional use. eBook versions and licenses are also available for most titles. For more information, reference our Print and eBook Bulk Sales web page at www.apress.com/bulk-sales.

Any source code or other supplementary material referenced by the author in this book is available to readers on GitHub (https://github.com/Apress). For more detailed information, please visit www.apress.com/source-code.

Printed on acid-free paper

I dedicate this book to all the people who journeyed with me (and are still here), my cofounders in previous startups, my current cofounder, Martina, and my friends and mentors.

Table of Contents

About the Author xi

About the Contributors xiii

Acknowledgments xvii

Foreword by Bruno Balen (Cidrani) xix

Introduction xxiii

Chapter 1: Look Around You 1
  What's So Special About Being a European Startup? 1
  We're Not All Living in America! (Yet!) 3
  How Not to Be a Prophet in Your Village 4
  Choosing a Problem to Solve/Build Your Business On 7
  It's All About the Gaps 11
  Service Businesses Need Not Apply 13
  What Type of Company Do You Need? 14
  The Corporate Veil 15

Chapter 2: Guest Chapter: A Founder's Guide Through the Legal Jungle 19
  Sharing and Protecting Ideas 20
  Great! You Have a Cofounder and Now You Need to Regulate Your Relationship 21
  When to Incorporate the Company 22
  How to Choose the Type of Legal Entity 23
  How to Take Investments 25

TABLE OF CONTENTS

Chapter 3: Setting Goals 29
    What's Not a Startup? 29
    What's a Stealth-Mode Startup? 30
    What Do Startups Do? 31
    Everyone Wants Recurring Revenue 32
    What's a Successful Startup? 34
    Staying Afloat 36
    When Does a Startup Stop Being a Startup? 36
    How to Approach the Market 37
    The Lifecycle of a VC-Backed Company 38
    On Hedging 40
    Who Buys European Startups? 41

Chapter 4: Guest Chapter: On the Franchise Model for Startups 43
    Why Franchise Your Concept 44
        Other Reasons 46
    Four Steps to a Successful Franchise 47
        Step 1: Create Something Successful, Profitable, and Scalable 47
        Step 2: Make It Desirable (to Entrepreneurs) 48
        Step 3: Work with an Expert Who Will Set Up Your Franchise Model 48
        Step 4: Start Saying "No" As Quickly As Possible 50
    What Are the Revenue Streams in a Franchise? 50
        A Summary Example 52
    When Does a Franchise Become Interesting to Investors and Potential Buyers? 53
        Summary: Focus on Internal Processes First 56
    Startups as Franchises 56

TABLE OF CONTENTS

Chapter 5: Getting Money 59
Equity and the Cap Table 59
Ways of Getting Money 60
A Special Note about EU and Governmental Funds 62
What Are Investors and What Do They Want? 64
Types of Investors 66
Investors Also Have Preferences 69
How to Deal with VC Funds 70
Finding Investors 73
What to Ask Money For 73
Red Flags in Investors 75
What to Spend Money On 76
What Is This Mysterious "Runway" Everyone Is Talking About? 77
The Financial Lifecycle of a Typical VC-Backed Unicorn Startup 80
Rules of the Game 84
When Diligence Is Due 87
The Eastern European Perspective on Company Shares 87
How Can Founders Make Money? 89

Chapter 6: Guest Chapter: On Startup Valuations (and Other Dark Stories) 93
The 5W Rule 94
Who? 94
Where? 95
What? 95
When? 96

vii

TABLE OF CONTENTS

Valuation 96
The Term Sheet 98
Conclusion 99

Chapter 7: Your Company is the Average of Its Founders 101

If You Need to Make Mistakes in Choosing Cofounders, Be Aware of Them in Advance 102
Corporate Culture Is Made of Founders' Habits 104
Remote Work Is Like a Potent Spice. Use It Sparingly 106
On Transparency 107
The Option Pool and Vesting 108
Waiting for ESOP in Europe 109

Chapter 8: Guest Chapter: Recruiting in a Startup Environment 113

Recruiting Starts Well Before the Recruiting Actually Starts 114
If You Talk the Talk, Walk the Walk 115
Recruiting From Personal Channels 116
No-Bullshit Job Descriptions 116
    Describe the Startup 117
    Describe the Position 117
    List Expectations of the Candidate 118
    Describe What the Startup Is Offering the Candidate 118
    Describe the Interview Process 119
Communication with Candidates 119
    Task Before the Interview 119
    Interview Process 120
    Onboarding 121
    Feedback Loop 123

Easy to Hire, Easy to Fire 123
Stock Options 124
Conclusion 124

Chapter 9: Managing Money 127
The Root of All Evil 127
Time Is Money 129
Reinvest Everything 130
The Holy Grail of the EBITDA Margin 131
On Growth 133

Chapter 10: Get Your Product Out There 137
Business Development 137
Pricing Strategies 139
Selling B2B vs. Selling B2C 141
Growth Hacking 142
Survival of the Most Tenacious 144
Use ChatGPT and Other Content Generators Where You Can 148

Chapter 11: The Big Exit Theory 151
Keep Your Head On 151
What If You Succeed? 152
Building for an Exit 154
Define "Win" 156

Chapter 12: Find Your Replacement(s) 159

Index 161

About the Author

Ivan Voras earned his PhD in Computer Engineering from the University of Zagreb Faculty of Electrical Engineering and Computing. He is an entrepreneur with a passion for exotic technologies. As a top-down architect and implementer of big IT systems, he worked on early blockchain products in 2014, IoT hardware in 2017, and is now a founder of startup Equinox Vision, which commercializes augmented reality.

Ivan is also a co-host of Croatia's biggest business and lifestyle podcast, *Surove Strasti*, and the startup-oriented *Well Founded* podcast. He was an associate editor for Croatia's biggest IT magazine, *Mreža*, from 2005 -2020. His passion is exploring the edge where technology meets real lives.

About the Contributors

Marijana Šarolić Robić is a tech-loving lawyer who found her passion for technology in 2013 when she joined ZIP (Zagreb Entrepreneurship Incubator) as a mentor. Since then she has mentored more than 100 startups, using her experience from her banking and finance background to support and advise founders in different stages of business development. Marijana is especially interested in AI and ethics, and she serves as the VP of CRO STARTUP, an association that promotes the Croatian startup ecosystem. She is a frequent cohost of the *Well Founded* podcast.

Andrija Andy Čolak is the founder of the Surf'n'Fries brand, the biggest F&B franchise from Croatia, now operating in over 20 countries all over the globe. He is founder of the CFCG consulting company and a franchising pioneer in this part of the world, with over a decade of practical experience in international franchise operations.

He was the winner of the NextGen award in 2015 in Las Vegas for the best young franchise manager under 35, awarded for a new franchise concept from the IFA (International Franchise Association), the world's biggest franchiser organization.

ABOUT THE CONTRIBUTORS

Božidar Pavlović, despite his computer science education, has extensive banking experience, having spent more than 20 years in retail banking (namely payments), mostly as COO, CTO, and eventually CEO. In the last ten years, his interests have turned towards Fintech and its evident ability to disrupt banking. Ultimately, he decided to investigate Fintech as an emerging trend first-hand, initially by seed investing and then by fully changing his career scope. Thus he joined an internationally acclaimed SaaS fintech startup as the CTO. Afterwards, he started his own boutique consultancy company, Jackie Agency. He also speaks at various conferences and sporadically lectures at various tech universities. He is also a mentor in a number of Croatian tech incubators and is an active board member of the CRO STARTUP association.

Mario Mucalo is a full stack developer with over 15 years of experience in the IT industry. He is the founder and CEO of Intellegens (a software development company) and CTO of the startup Peekator (a market research platform for true market researchers). He worked first as a developer at Lemax, a Croatian company producing one of the top five software solutions for tour operators and DMCs, but later moved to technical presales. He also worked for Toptal, the world's top network of freelance experts, first as a freelance software developer, and later became the Director of Engineering and Head of the Technical Screening team.

ABOUT THE CONTRIBUTORS

Mario is enthusiastic about sharing his knowledge, which is why you can find him speaking at conferences, participating in events such as the Startup Factory Accelerator from ZICER, and writing his own blog. This is also how he came to be associated with this book! Every now and then you can find him on a basketball court or behind a drum set.

Acknowledgments

I have many people to thank for making this book possible and for sticking with me even when the book seemed a pipe dream. First, I'd like to thank the contributing writers: Marijana Šarolić Robić, Andrija Čolak, Božidar Pavlović, and Mario Mucalo: without your expertise and reality checks, it would have been much harder to put the book together. I'd also like to thank Saša Tenodi, my podcasting co-host in the biggest business and lifestyle audio podcast in the region, *Surove Strasti*, for enduring my stubbornness and for being there as we learned from our guests. Finally, I'm grateful to my fiancé, Diana, who has been there through ups and downs.

Foreword by Bruno Balen (Cidrani)

IS THERE A MANUAL FOR THE IMPOSSIBLE?

"It would be so much easier to build a successful startup if I were doing it in the US."

This is a sentence I hear a lot, and paradoxically I believe it embodies the hidden threat within the CEE region's startup mentality.

Building a startup and going against all odds is not a shiny trend that started in the Valley, reserved for the chosen ones with perfect Californian accents. It is engraved in the fabric of the collective DNA that makes us humans.

That burning desire to achieve what seems impossible is what we all share with the great leader Marcus Aurelius, brave Spartans, mighty Alexander, and genius Tesla. They didn't choose the safe path and did not have a manual.

I haven't had one either. I am proud and happy to see that, finally, there is a manual that can help founders prevent at least some mistakes.

This "cookbook" serves as a meta-tool to help all of us avoid mistakes others have made, and as such, it is invaluable.

It shows that the scene is maturing, and I am excited to see the genius solutions coming from our region straight to the global throne.

I would have given the world to have had such a manual when we were starting, and I am honored to be part of this through sharing at least some of the inspiration and passion I found in this endeavor.

I also want to emphasize the feeling of discomfort and the slaps and punches I received (and still receive daily) when facing the conversation with reality, without any guidance.

Here are the five things I wish I had known before I embarked on this journey:

1) **It won't be easy. Take it stoically.**

   Marcus Aurelius taught his pupils that it was never supposed to be easy, but that we can and must find a way to withstand every storm.

2) **Embrace purpose over comfort. Together.**

   Spartans were left to survive on their own in the wilderness before they became warriors. However, they didn't fight alone. It is people's business, so invest in finding the best ones to share your mission with.

3) **Never give up. Ever.**

   In four voyages, Columbus lost nine ships and kept going. Long before he "discovered" the Valley, he was a true startupper. There is no chance a person won't succeed in their intention if they persist and don't give up. It is only a matter of time.

4) **Focus. Let go of the unnecessary. "Kill Darius."**

   When Alexander the Great faced the mighty Persian army, which outnumbered his, he focused on a single target: their king, Darius. And succeeded. Set big goals for five years from now and find a way to do them in six months. This will help you discard what holds you back.

5) **Be patient. Be impatient.**

> Tesla made it to the US in 1884, powered by a vast vision. He died 59 years later without executing it until the end. The speed of learning, pivoting, and changing how to achieve your dream is not to be compromised. Be patient with your bold vision but be impatient with the pace at which you achieve it.

No, it is not possible.

But one thing is for sure . . . with *The European VC-Funded Startup Guide*, it will be slightly less impossible.

About Bruno:

Bruno is a true startupper. His only jobs have been working in the companies he founded. That gave him the freedom to experiment and learn about his true passions; biohacking, longevity, and extended levels of vitality.

*Over the last ten years, he has travelled to more than 45 countries and invested more than 6000 hours into educating himself on how to stay younger and healthier. In the process, he fell in love with gut microbiota and, together with his partner, Nika, co-founded Ani Biome (*https://anibiome.ai/*), a Croatian LaaS (longevity as a service) startup that aims to eradicate aging and become the number one agetech company worldwide. In the last twelve months, Ani Biome has grown their team by five times, achieved three times growth in revenue, and opened a new lab and production facility in Zagreb. They have also won first place at the AI2Future Startup Competition and the Firmenich Precision Nutrition Demo Day, gold for the most innovative product at Organic Iberia Madrid, the Unicorn Award at the Infobip Shift conference, and first place at EIT ClimAccelerator Beyond.*
genius@anibiome.ai

Introduction

> **TL;DR**
>
> - Each chapter will begin with a "TL;DR" section like this.
> - This book is meant for those just starting as first-time founders.
> - It's especially important to read this book if all or most of your education is from US-centric advice and materials.
> - Read it again a year into your startup journey.

Who Should Read This Book?

Short answer: Someone who's just beginning to think about forming their first startup located in Europe. Then, the very same person about a year into the whole ordeal.

But it doesn't normally go that way. Many of us, myself included, search for solutions when we encounter a problem; it's more time-efficient that way, at least in the short term. And really, you don't have as much time as you think.

In terms of reader profiles, I think this book is not terribly useful to people already experienced in business, who have already started one or more successful companies that employ multiple people. Other than that, most people who have an interest in startups and the associated ecosystem, especially in Europe, will find something interesting here.

INTRODUCTION

Who Wrote This Book?

The principal author is me, Ivan Voras. Unless otherwise stated, if the text is using a direct voice to talk to you, it is my train of thought behind it.

I have a PhD in computer engineering and so far I've been a scientist, a journalist for the two biggest IT magazines in Croatia (*BUG* and *Mreža*), I have participated in large global open source projects (including being a kernel/core developer for FreeBSD), and I've been a freelancer highly specialized in exotic technologies, including the blockchain and IoT, back when they were new.

I am currently a founder and CEO of the augmented reality platform (metaverse as a service) startup named Equinox Vision, and much of the knowledge I present in this book comes from my direct experiences with this startup, as I develop it in the context of its domicile country of Croatia, in Eastern Europe.

I'm not the only author, though. I have asked some of my colleagues who are experts in certain areas to contribute chapters on specific topics. In no particular order, they are

- Marijana Šarolić Robić, an attorney specializing in startup affairs
- Andrija Čolak, owner of the Surf'n'Fries franchise and a franchise consultant
- Božidar Pavlović, an investor and VC manager
- Mario Mucalo, an entrepreneur with a history in companies specializing in recruiting, the CEO and owner of Intellegens and the CTO at Peekator

I wish to send them warm thanks for their support, advice, and contributions to this book. It would have been much harder without them.

INTRODUCTION

We Need to Agree on Something: What Is a "Startup?"

There are a lot of definitions out there. I side with the one that says *a startup is a young company that is creating a product, aiming for the global market and fast growth.*

This fast growth is usually accomplished by acquiring a lot of funding to fuel it, and the most common way of gathering a lot of funding is through VCs. Startups walk the VC-funded path simply because, in most cases, it takes a lot of quick capital to start growing fast.

There are two poorly defined concepts here: how fast is "fast growth" and how much money is needed for it? Both are hard to define, although there are some rules of thumb that usually influence the perception of the two:

- Usually, especially for bureaucratic purposes in the EU, a "young" company is less than five years old (although this can vary depending on the program and even between member countries). If a startup doesn't start to show fast growth (it doesn't need to be hockey-stick growth, but it needs to be visible) within five years, it won't necessarily stop calling itself a "startup," but it will eventually become awkward to do so.

- Usually, revenue and number of employees don't matter on the global scale, though again, the EU has its own criteria[1], which are usually good enough: the SME category (small and medium enterprises) encompasses every company with fewer than 250 employees and less than €50 million turnover, which is plenty for startups.

---

[1] Erasmus for Young entrepreneurs, www.erasmus-entrepreneurs.eu/page.php?cid=6&pid=019&faqcat=14&faqid=101.

INTRODUCTION

- Software development requires much less capital than other industries, so there are a lot of investment opportunities that offer relatively small sums of money (less than €100,000) to develop a software startup MVP. Hardware is an order of magnitude more difficult prospect and out of the scope of this book.

- More than 60% of accelerators invested more than $1 million in their accelerated companies[2], usually through multiple rounds.

In the early days of the startup, you and your founding team will do everything, from actually working on a product (which will usually be the least of your worries) to paying bills to creating and vetting contracts to sweeping the floor of your office and taking out the garbage. Yes, this means you will certainly be doing stuff you have not trained for, have no affinity for, and probably hate doing.

How long these "early days" last depends on how well your business is doing. Fortunately (or not, depending on the view), the success of the startup does not strongly correlate to how long it takes for it to find the optimum path.

If that gets you (re)thinking your choices, you won't be happy with the next bit of information. It takes even longer for the founders to make an exit. Here are some examples: WhatsApp was founded in 2009 and bought by Facebook in 2014, a five-year time span. Roblox was started in 2004 and they IPO-ed in 2021, a staggering 17-year span. Not all of this time is spent in early-stage problems, of course.

Once you have reasonable revenue (to use deliberately unspecific wording), your startup will become a *scaleup*, meaning it's less of a question *if* it will succeed, but by *how much*.

---

[2] Emerald, *European Journal of Management and Business Economics*, Lydia Cánovas-Saiz, Isidre March-Chordà, Rosa Maria Yagüe-Perales, "New evidence on accelerator performance based on funding and location," www.emerald.com/insight/content/doi/10.1108/EJMBE-10-2017-0029/full/html#sec004

INTRODUCTION

Does this mean that if you're not aiming for global domination and haven't drunk the Kool-Aid of Peter Thiel's *Zero to One*[3] (whether you agree with him or not, it's a book you should read), what you're doing isn't a startup?

It depends.

There certainly are companies that don't fit my preferred startup definition but have gathered both popularity and investments and operate as nice, profitable, local-ish businesses. Some of them later decided to go global and have succeeded. Of course, there are some that failed miserably and would have fared better if they stayed local.

I'll introduce another criterion here that isn't supposed to be used as a differentiator of what's a startup but often is, *is the business a VC case?* By "VC case," I mean if it would and should be backed by VCs. This boils down to whether the return-on-investment calculations hit a certain (high) mark in a (short) number of years. I'll talk about this more in later chapters.

One More Thing: Do You Need VC Money?

While having money to develop your idea into a product GREATLY reduces stress and time to market (and after all, time is money), do think twice before you go this route. Unless what you are doing is a very high-tech product that simply cannot be developed without an army of experts or requires a large money chest at start for some other legitimate reason, it could be better in the long term if you at least try to do it without a VC investment. To paraphrase an influential TechCrunch article[4], VC money

---

[3] Peter Thiel, *Zero to One: Notes on Startups, or How to Build the Future* (New York, NY: Crown, 2014)

[4] Tech Crunch, Joseph Flaherty, "Invisible unicorns: 35 big companies that started with little or no money," https://techcrunch.com/2017/07/01/invisible-unicorns-35-big-companies-that-started-with-little-or-no-money/

itself will not make your product great, or desired, and certainly will not make you happy.

If you decide the VC route is the best for you, I hope this book will help you navigate the (sometimes literally) treacherous waters and get out of the ordeal in a better shape than you were while getting into it.

PERSONAL EXAMPLE #1: IS IT A (SERIOUS) STARTUP?

My first startup-like experience was when I got together with a group of friends and enthusiastically drew up a plan to create "smart city furniture." It was a hardware business and a reason why we got into it was that one of us had a family business of creating traffic signs and similar street furniture. We were baffled as to why no one treated us seriously but I can now point out what was wrong with this concept:

- The hardware business is much, much harder than software, and none of us had real experience producing hardware on a large scale.

- We didn't have an expansive plan. We were always trying to satisfy the needs of the local or at most the country-wide market.

- We didn't even try to get external funding to improve our chances. We were convinced that at the time, our Eastern European country didn't have any funding options, and more importantly, we thought we didn't have anyone to ask for advice.

Unsurprisingly, the business fell apart, with some friendships lost. If I were to summarize all that in a single sentence, the main reason was that we underestimated how complex each and every aspect of the business was, and have overvalued our uniqueness.

PERSONAL EXAMPLE #2: DO WE NEED VC MONEY?

One piece of advice that is implicit in all VC-funded deals but for obvious reasons is seldom spoken aloud is, *never gamble with your own money*. The ideal position for creating a startup is if you arrive at a situation in life where you have access to money that will not be missed if gone, and you are highly skilled in a segment of an industry where you clearly see changes or improvements can be made.

In later chapters, I'll talk about what actually happens when you accept VC money, but for now, I'd say that with my Equinox Vision startup we accepted the tiny pre-seed investment too early, which means we gave up a relatively big chunk of equity, and the investment didn't help much to get the company going.

Doing it again, I'd seriously consider waiting until we had a first client before accepting any investment. Of course, this is hard and means a lot of development must be bootstrapped.

CHAPTER 1

Look Around You

TL;DR

- Do not found a startup to solve a purely local problem.
- But, unless you have the resources and skill to go global immediately, you must find your initial customers locally.
- Do not blindly trust books, blogs, and media from the US if your company is based in Europe.
- Build a product, not a service.
- Know the difference between your clients and your users.

What's So Special About Being a European Startup?

The startup concept originated in the US, which has two indispensable benefits over most of the rest of the world:

- A huge domestic market that is simultaneously extremely well developed, rich, and open to new opportunities

CHAPTER 1   LOOK AROUND YOU

- A cultural domination over most of the world through the English language, entertainment, and social media products

On the other hand, the European market (and in this book I'm talking about the continent, not only the EU) is pretty much the opposite. It is a fragmented market with very different rates of economic and cultural progress, and very different cultures can be found bordering each other.

The European Union did a lot to homogenize the market. The introduction of the Euro currency and the free traffic of goods and people within the Schengen borders (including, notably, removing any import duties and fees for goods within the EU) are huge benefits that are a necessary part of how EU member countries operate nowadays, but it's often not enough. Countries have different legal systems, some of them have retained their sovereign currencies, and almost all of them have their own language and a unique culture.

Due to historical happenings, most European countries have not implemented capitalism to the extent that the US has. Many countries have no mechanisms with which they can attract people into becoming investors or business founders, and there can be non-trivial barriers to establishing and running an internationally operating business.

Even going past all that, investors in Europe are simply often of a smaller caliber than what can be found in the hotspots of the US, notably San Francisco and New York. I'll talk more about this issue later.

All of this means that European startups are often forced to take different paths than those in the US, and there's a severe lack of available information on how to do that. This book aims to at least start rectifying that problem.

CHAPTER 1   LOOK AROUND YOU

We're Not All Living in America! (Yet!)

The band Rammstein did a very good satirical music video on this topic, and I'm borrowing their lyrics for this section's title. You would be doing yourself a favor by seeing "Amerika" by Rammstein[1].

There are significant differences between what you can learn on social media and forums and in seminars, conferences, and books that are targeted towards the US market versus what is currently (as of 2023) possible in Europe. This is true no matter what part of Europe you are in, and EU membership has little to do with it.

An exception in this region is the UK, and they're trying hard not to be considered a part of Europe, for which I have some sympathy, because the EU is definitely getting dragged down by its own bureaucracy.

Most of the "startup hustler" mindset is only valid (meaning: productive) in a small number of high-powered areas, such as Silicon Valley, London, New York, and Seattle, and it boils down to the amount of money circulating around. Compared to the Hollywood film industry, Silicon Valley absolutely dominates with the net worth of its companies. Walt Disney Studios is currently (Q1 2023) worth about $130 billion and is the world's largest "studio" (they bought a large number of smaller companies relatively recently), while Sony Pictures is worth about $105 billion. You'd need about 20 of such studios to approach Apple's market cap, which is around $2500 billion. If money is being discussed, the Silicon Valley is the place to be.

I'll try to explain the major difference with the following metaphor. An (individual) investor in those high-powered areas tends to think in the terms of, *Do I invest in your company, or do I buy myself a third Bentley?* while an investor in most of the rest of the world, including pretty much the entire continent of Europe, thinks in the terms of, *Will I screw up my retirement if I invest in your risky business?*

---

[1] YouTube, "Rammstein, Amerika," www.youtube.com/watch?v=Rr8ljRgcJNM

CHAPTER 1   LOOK AROUND YOU

Another difference is in the scaling mindset. US-based investors in high-powered areas view startups as rocket-fueled businesses whose job is to carve out a significant market share as quickly as possible. This is done by offering users something they like, locking them in, and then figuring out a way to extract money out of this large mass of users. In a market of more than 330 million just in the US, and more than a billion in the total English-speaking world, extracting a couple of dollars from a large market share is all it takes for a business to be lauded as successful.

European investors are much more cautious. Since there's no large mono-cultural market, especially because of all the different languages (there's a reason you're reading this in English), they concentrate on forcing the startups to earn money as soon as possible, even if that method is suboptimal, just to guard themselves against ideas that are too "blue sky" (too difficult) to implement in the domicile environment.

This has become the main reason for the lack of VC-funded unicorns in Europe. Those who succeeded often did so without VC investments since they recognized early that the "bad kind" of VCs would be actively detrimental to their business.

Consider this seriously: the US is a market of 330 million people speaking the same language. If you expand that to the whole English-speaking world, that's about a billion people. Compare that to your country. As soon as there's an indication people want to buy your product, go global.

How Not to Be a Prophet in Your Village

What follows is very conditional advice. On one hand, succeeding in your native environment might result in establishing strong business roots which could support a large business later. This is especially true if you are building your first "real" startup (with a realistic chance of succeeding globally) and need a familiar base to learn from. On the other hand, solving problems in small and/or poor markets might not be the right path if you are aiming for global or more affluent markets.

Starting small in Europe or choosing to solve a problem typical of your local-ish environment might make you blind to the opportunities available in international markets because of the simple fact that the day-to-day business might be so demanding that you simply don't have the time and resources to pay attention.

Because of all the cultural and language hurdles, it might be better to spend as little time in your starting European country as possible, and it can be argued that this phase should end before you receive any external funding. While there are cases where European startups got appropriately funded and their headquarters remained in their home country, they are rare. As I'll later show, the simple fact is that at the time of writing this book, the quality of most European investors is really low and, consequently, funding is of low quality and intensity.

It's more typical that *bootstrapped* startups, which succeed in getting to international markets before receiving VC funding, remain in their starting countries, taking advantage of the cheaper cost of living.

VC-funded Eastern European startups that have succeeded have typically relocated to a more business-hospitable country like the US, the UK, Singapore, Korea, or even Israel when they received their first serious funding round.

This doesn't mean you need to physically relocate, at least not for some time, but it is very advisable for the company HQ to be in a jurisdiction that has clear trade laws, functioning IP protection, and a fast legislature.

CHAPTER 1   LOOK AROUND YOU

Key benefits to moving to a startup-friendly country include:

- Not being subject to messed-up courts, tax, and work laws

- Operating in an environment that already has a lot of experience with startups and can handle your company in a standardized, templated way (which significantly reduces costs and legal friction)

- Having access to better investors who are more willing to work with startups located in friendly environments with less legal and business risk. Even European investors are often more willing to invest in US companies because of this.

That said, if you keep your business in the EU, you might (but with a very large dose of uncertainty, from personal experience) be able to benefit from

- Financial and social safety nets, and the support of your friends and family

- EU funding. This topic is worth its own section in Chapter 5.

In any case, unless your business relies on or exploits a particular feature of the European physical, legislative, or cultural landscape, you should probably establish or move your business somewhere startup-friendly. The state of Delaware in the US is a very common destination. It will not solve all your problems, but it will solve enough of them to allow you to concentrate on the more important ones.

CHAPTER 1   LOOK AROUND YOU

Choosing a Problem to Solve/Build Your Business On

One thing is very true: if you are starting a global business just for the money, you will soon find out that money is not a strong enough motivation.

This is a very difficult idea to process, and it is worth some deep thought. In the vast majority of cases, the process of starting a business with global ambitions is difficult enough that sooner or later most people say to themselves something to the tune of, "I'm not paid enough for this shit."

In addition to finding something profitable to do, you also need to be very passionate about doing it, often unreasonably so. It's very normal to have periods of time when the only way to sleep at all is by clinging to your vision of the world with your product in it.

If you are going down the VC-funded route to start a business (and you probably are if you're reading this book), then you want the product you're creating to be globally useful right from the start. You might not have the money to market the product globally yet, or a clue on how to do it in the next three years, but the product must be scalable in an obvious way from day 1. The reason for this is simple: investors want a quick turnaround on their money.

However, if this is your first startup (or even second or third) and if you're based in Europe (especially Eastern Europe), what do you know of what a customer in New York needs? As with any creative field, you always work with what you know.

All European VCs I've encountered will flatly tell you two contradictory things:

1) your business needs to be globally scalable and

2) you need to validate the business idea locally (because it's cheaper).

CHAPTER 1   LOOK AROUND YOU

It is up to you to solve this Gordian Knot of conditions.

Solving a local problem might paint you into a corner where you eventually discover that most of the world doesn't have this problem. On the other hand, starting with a big, global idea could lead you into a situation where there are not enough customers for you locally to even get the business going, and VCs won't show up unless they see customers.

Even if you find a neat, well-defined problem to solve by building a new product, the existence of a solution *in theory* does not imply the existence of a solution *in practice*. Additionally, the existence of a solution in practice does not mean that you, specifically, will be able to pull it off.

Another aspect of choosing the business to work on is who your customers will be, whether B2B, B2C, or something else. Just to reiterate:

- **B2B**: Your business sells to other businesses.

- **B2C**: Your business sells directly to customers/consumers/regular people.

- **B2B2C**: Your business sells to other businesses which resell/repackage the product to sell directly to customers.

- **B2G**: Your business sells directly to government(s).

A sad but true story is that in most of the world (including in the US), the best market to be in is B2G. But the problems governments have are usually boring, bureaucratized, or questionably ethical. If all you want is loads of money, sell something to the defense departments.

To get a sense of how these business models look in practice, here are some real-world examples. If it surprises you to find out what these businesses actually do, you might think again about if you are ready to start a business.

- **Facebook/Meta** (including Instagram, WhatsApp, and other properties): B2B. It sells absolutely nothing directly to end users.

- **Amazon**: B2B, B2C. Amazon does buy and hold a certain amount of its own inventory, and that gets them into the B2C category, but just barely. The vast majority of what Amazon does is pure B2B, since it offers services (digital storefronts, fulfilment, and others) to other businesses.

- **Google**: B2B, B2C. It sells almost nothing directly to end users; the notable exceptions are subscriptions to YouTube, disk space for Google Photos and Drive, and a small volume of mobile phones.

- **Apple**: B2C, B2B. Contrary to Google, it sells a lot directly to end users, but it makes even more money by taking fees from App Store developers (B2B).

- **Telecoms**: B2B, B2C, B2G. Telecoms connect end users and businesses, but recently they have also earned a fair amount from government surveillance actions.

- **Netflix**: B2C. It doesn't sell to other businesses.

- **Ubisoft**, **Blizzard**, **EPIC Games**, etc. (game developers): B2C, B2B. They sell their product (games) directly to end users, but they also increasingly take money from third-party businesses for product placement and ads. The movie industry is similar.

- **McDonald's**: B2B, B2B2C. The parent company is practically a real estate company; 93% of McDonald's stores are franchises, and the parent company does next to nothing directly with B2C anymore. See the chapter on franchises later in this book for more information.

CHAPTER 1 LOOK AROUND YOU

It's immediately obvious that your *clients* might not be—and for long-running companies usually are not—your *users*.

Clients pay you money. Users actively use your product. This is a subtle thing to pay attention to, even in situations where it should be clear-cut. If you are selling B2B, it is *very important* to realize that the people paying for your product are usually not the ones who end up using it, and in some cases might not be aware of their needs.

To win repeat customers, you ideally satisfy the needs of both groups (even if their needs are divergent), but in practice, being on friendly terms with the ones who sign buying orders is often enough.

A worn-out mantra says that starting a business only makes sense if it solves a problem that someone will pay to have solved. Let's elaborate on that thought quickly.

Should you go for B2B or B2C? If going for B2B, your primary goal, which you should probably write down on a sticker and stick it on the ceiling so you see it every time you wake up in your bed, should be, *How does my product help my (potential) clients to earn more money?*

If you are after B2C, you have a little more leeway, but for a global startup it always comes down to doing something that touches on the first (bottom) levels of the Maslow's pyramid of needs, simply because those things are common to the widest possible set of potential clients. In the context of B2C, you should probably create something that helps solve issues relating to air, water, food, housing, clothing, sex, personal safety (including legal compliance), employment, health, property, friendship, communication, belonging, or fun. Anything outside of this list is best viewed as a bonus and is probably not a good primary goal.

Like Paul Graham[2] said (you should follow him and read his articles), "The way to get startup ideas is not to try to think of startup ideas. It's to look for problems…" Do not sit around in chill cafes trying to brainstorm startup ideas. Instead of brainstorming, go ask people to describe their

---

[2] Paul Graham, "How to get startup ideas," www.paulgraham.com/startupideas.html

problems and see if you are also passionate about some of them. You have probably heard it said that you should build a product you yourself want to buy, and this is usually a good advice, but in that case, you really need to know how many like-minded people there are in the world (i.e. how many potential customers you would have).

This is the difference between being an *inventor* and being a *businessman*. An inventor will often build something they think is cool. A businessman will always run away from ideas they don't see how to sell to other people.

It's All About the Gaps

Everything in the universe happens at gaps (or gradients), places where stuff that has a high amount of something meets stuff that has a lower amount of the same thing. In chemistry, things happen when particles high in energy meet particles low in energy. If you put two low-energy particles together, or two high-energy particles together, nothing happens.

Business happens when people (or companies) who possess the capability, knowledge, or capital meet other people (or companies) who do not.

If you met your twin in intellect, world view, resources, career, but also flaws, you would most probably soon become bored with them, because you would agree on everything but also have the same blind spots. Either that or you would both decide to operate as a single unit from now on—but you couldn't hire each other. If every person on Earth had exactly the same capabilities, everyone would be paid exactly the same, because no one would accept lower pay.

I tend to think of money the same way physicists think of energy: work can be done only where there's a gap in money. The more money is spread across the globe, the more the standard of living is raised for the workers, and the higher salary they will demand. Unless physics or mammalian politics interfere, the theoretical end game of globalism is a zero entropy situation, where everyone has the same amount of money and the same living standard.

In practical terms, businesses thrive if they have something their surroundings want: that's the gap. The two most impactful types of gaps are

- **Information gap**: Some businesses have better information than others.
- **Capability gap**: Some businesses are more capable in a certain area than others.

Richness in information also covers innovation—but in that case, it's always combined with the foresight that that particular innovation is just what the market wants *right now*. You could very easily innovate a battery-powered mousetrap with lasers and expect a market of billions, but the simple fact that people don't want to change its batteries every week would make this product flop in the market. A company that does the same basic product but 15 years into the future when batteries are much more powerful than today will succeed.

Capability is the hardest thing to achieve, and it's the hardest to plan and predict. People usually covet and admire capability. Many people who are into martial arts or high-performance training don't want or need to fight or run for their lives, but they have the *capability* to do so on demand, and we admire them for it.

But people can easily be deluded into believing that they possess a capability (e.g., bodybuilders) and many times fail miserably when an actual need (e.g., a fight) happens. It's the same with companies. It's hard to predict if a company flexing in the spotlight got there because of the capability of their funders or due to plain luck. (To be honest, sometimes plain luck is enough.)

The product design takeaway here is to find something you can do which is reasonably unique but also sellable. If you are doing what everyone else does, at least do it in a new and interesting way. Find something your company can produce or possess but that your local (and especially global) environment wants.

Service Businesses Need Not Apply

It's all about scalability. Service businesses sell the expertise of their employees, usually in the form of hours of labor. A marketing agency might use the same tools and have the same basic structure for different campaigns and different clients, but still, people need to create those campaigns and all the materials for them. A bakery is in the same category: despite all the machinery, you need people to make bread and pastries, and then sell them.

This is in contrast to having a well-defined, differentiated product, which only you make and sell, and which is sold without customization to a very wide set of customers[3]. This cookie-cutter product business can grow more by adding more machinery and raw materials than by adding workers.

The software industry is the shining example of this. The Software-as-a-Service businesses, such as those based on offering cloud/web apps, grow by adding servers, which can be maintained by a small team of skilled workers. Such a company can grow by 10 to 30 times and not hire a single additional worker. Investors like that. They like it so much that they specifically look for that pattern in potential businesses they are willing to invest in.

---

[3] Keep in mind the difference between customers and clients. For someone to be your customer, it's enough for them to pay you once for something. With clients, you will hopefully develop a long-term relationship.

CHAPTER 1   LOOK AROUND YOU

If your business needs to hire people for each new parallel client you sign up, it does not fit this pattern. Often, just the opposite is true: service businesses are the ones buying products from startups and using them as tools for their business. You know the saying: in a gold rush, it's best to be the one who sells shovels. You do not want to be an Uber driver. You want to be Uber. You do not want to be the guy generating marketing slogans from an AI, you want to build that AI.

What Type of Company Do You Need?

If you are planning for a startup—which I've defined as a fast-growing global business, usually backed by VC funding—you will sooner or later need to form (or transform into) a type of company that can issue shares. Some of the names of this type of business across Europe (with reference to the US) are

- English (Great Britain): Public Limited Company (PLC)
- English (US): Corporation (Inc.)
- Slovenian: Delniška družba (d.d.)
- Croatian: Dioničko društvo (d.d.)
- Italian: Società per azioni (S.A.)
- Romanian: Societate pe Acțiuni (S.A.)
- French: Société anonyme (S.A.)
- Polish: Spółka Akcyjna (S.A.)
- Dutch: Naamloze vennootschap (N.V.)
- German: Aktiengesellschaft (AG)
- Estonian: Aktsiaselts (AS)

- Latvian: Akciju sabiedrība (AS)
- Bulgarian: Акционерно дружество (AD)
- Ukrainian: Акціонерне товариство (AT)

In many East European countries, establishment and bookkeeping operations of this type of company are costly and often discouraged, mostly because the laws are not compatible with the idea that there can exist a share-issuing company that employs only a couple of people. Typically, there's a mountain of paperwork and audits to endure, and there might be a significant entry fee for company creation (named something like "base capital"). I will talk more about this later.

In this situation, you should probably form a limited liability company (LLC), but the legislature across European countries varies very wildly about what forms of ownership, rights, and transactions are possible with them. Again, it's better to form a company in more developed countries, like Ireland, the Netherlands, and the UK. Germany is an outlier here as a developed country with an overwhelmingly rigid bureaucracy, and you probably don't want that.

The Corporate Veil

The concept of a corporation came about because society at large noticed there is a substantial benefit to allowing people to do risky businesses (such as sailing to distant lands in search of spices and jewels), while at the same time shielding them from at least some of the bad things that can happen which are not their fault (such as storms, pirates, and sea monsters). The British East India Company is considered the first such entity, incorporated in the year 1600 (followed closely by the Dutch equivalent, the VOC, in 1602).

CHAPTER 1   LOOK AROUND YOU

Because such entities need to have capabilities that natural persons have by default, such as the ability to own things, represent themselves in court, and such, a new idea was formed, that of a "corporate person" (a.k.a. a judicial person), which is a term often synonymous with "corporation." This also applies to LLCs (limited liability companies).

Corporations, as their name suggests, are, in a weird way, treated as people and are separate from their owners (a.k.a. the shareholders). In some countries, corporations have the same type and form of official ID number as natural persons. While natural persons normally receive this number when they are born, corporations receive it when they are created (incorporated).

This is very important: the corporation and its owners are two different things. The corporation's director can represent the corporation where needed, but there are limits as to what they can do. For example, they cannot use the corporation's money as if it were their own. The corporation, just as a natural person might do, needs to give its money away through some kind of contract. If someone who doesn't have the legal rights to do so uses the company's resources as if they were their own, they are held personally held responsible, and this event is called "piercing the corporate veil." Such directors are usually severely fined and even jailed.

The corporation might get into debt, but that debt does not normally transfer to the owners/shareholders. Unfortunately, especially for small companies, it's not unheard of that banks, other types of creditors, and leasing companies can demand that the owners/shareholders personally guarantee (underwrite) that the loan will be returned, possibly involving collateral. This is not how the system was designed to work, but on the other hand, it's a way for the creditors to protect themselves against people founding companies just to cause them to default on their debt.

The "corporate veil" concept is the reason why it is said that the interests of the corporation might not align with the interests of its founders, shareholders, or directors. Lawyers representing the company can, and will, unless otherwise instructed, craft legal documents that are beneficial to the company itself but detrimental to its founders.

> **PERSONAL EXAMPLE: YOU CANNOT TRUST POLLS/MARKET RESEARCH**
>
> Before we founded Equinox Vision, we wanted to make sure the idea was sound and that there would be customers interested in what we were aiming to build. So we interviewed people from a couple of tourist agencies and tourist boards, as well as some marketing agencies. We were apparently very good at describing the product since the answer was uniformly very positive. It was much later when we found out that we were also very ineffective in the way we did it, as that positive feedback did not translate into sales. It turned out the product was ahead of its time, and we needed to spend some time educating our customers about how our product could help them.

CHAPTER 2

Guest Chapter: A Founder's Guide Through the Legal Jungle

By Marijana Šarolić Robić

TL;DR
- You should be on friendly terms with a lawyer because you are going to need one. - You especially need a lawyer when you are dealing with a foreign business, including an investor. - Protecting your idea is usually not worth the effort in the early stages. The important thing is the *execution* of the idea. - Create a company only when you need one. If you can create a proof of concept or a minimum viable product without a company (i.e., without employees, etc.), do it that way.

CHAPTER 2 GUEST CHAPTER: A FOUNDER'S GUIDE THROUGH THE LEGAL JUNGLE

First of all, let's sort something out. I am a lawyer and I have been active in the Croatian startup community as a mentor since 2013. Therefore, I know a bit about law and the startup world. I have also founded a few startups myself that died rather early—one before the beta version was even out, and another one in the MVP stage. So, I also resonate with wearing a founder's hat - and emphatize.

The reasons why I chose to write this legal section of this startup cookbook are to help you through the legal jungle and ensure that it is as useful as possible and as close to the real-life experience one can get, even whan I'm giving blanket advice.

Please beware that this text is solely based on my experience as a startup lawyer, mentor, and/or founder, and serves only for information purposes. Any actual situation you are facing at the moment you are reading this must be taken to and discussed with professional advisers (attorney at law, tax consultant, business consultant, etc.). Only such professionals can have a clear perspective and address all layers of your situation properly.

Some information and advice given here is centered around Croatia, because I live and work there, but most of it is applicable to other Eastern European countries.

Sharing and Protecting Ideas

I always repeat what my MBA Entrepreneurship teacher Esteban Brenes used to say when it comes to ideas. Professor Brenes compared ideas with trains leaving the station. While ideas, like trains, come and go, we decide which train we will embark on and which destination we will reach. So, do not hold onto ideas; execution is crucial.

In my opinion, when it comes to idea sharing, I am a completely altruistic person. I share my ideas with different people, not just the ones who I know perceive the world as I do, but also the ones who perceive the world differently. The goal here is to get as many perspectives as possible and to mitigate the chance that my passion about an idea will prevent me from determining that the idea is not as great as I might perceive it.

I am never afraid that someone will steal my idea, knowing it is not possible to have the same execution of the same idea because we are all different and authentic humans. It is good to keep in mind that the idea itself cannot be protected by any intellectual property mechanism available.

So, when you have a wonderful business idea going through your head for days, do share it with others and listen to their perspective and feedback, especially if there are future customers among those people.

Great! You Have a Cofounder and Now You Need to Regulate Your Relationship

After talking to your friends, family, neighbors, experts, passers-by, and future customers, you have determined that you have an idea worth pursuing and you have decided to go for it. However, it might be that you do not have all the skills in your toolbox to develop such an idea, or maybe you just want to leverage the burden. So, you find a soulmate to share the journey with.

Now is the right moment to define your relationship and the milestones you want to achieve. My strong recommendation is to put it in writing. Any written form will do. Just define what each of you is bringing to the deal and how much time each of you will commit to spending on developing your joint startup. Simply set the timeframe and milestones and agree on actions. Put it on paper and sign it, even if it seems outdated, because the simple gesture of signing the final version of the document you draft together will support the validity of the deal and commit you to deliver much better than the spoken (and possibly misremembered) word.

A written document is also something you can go to when in doubt about what was agreed upon and it may help remind you of your other team members' promises for delivery. If the time test proves the idea was too ambitious or that maybe the team is not tackling all the challenges, the contract can always be amended and redrafted to fit your needs. But please do keep it in writing (even an email exchange will do).

Moreover, setting straight expectations and defining the strengths and resources you, as founders, have helps identify the things you lack in the execution of your vision. It also establishes an internal culture of dialogue, agreement, and transparency between founders.

I would even name such a written agreement as a basic shareholder agreement of the future company.

When to Incorporate the Company

So, you have tested that the idea is not completely useless by talking to people, you have found your cofounder(s), and you are thinking about incorporating a company. When is the right time to do it?

In my experience, you should incorporate the company only when you have already developed your beta product, or when you have a customer waiting to pay for your product. The reasons are as follows:

- Having a company and being a shareholder and director might be swell, but it costs time and money, no matter if you have any revenue or not.

- Once you incorporate the company under any jurisdiction, you will have some obligations as a shareholder and as a director (legal responsibilities, even tax responsibilities), so do learn about those things before entering the world of business ownership and management.

- Some businesses fail for various reasons, and in such cases, the companies must be dissolved or liquidated, and that also costs time and money.

How to Choose the Type of Legal Entity

Depending on your product or service, your customer profile, the environment you are operating in, and the markets you are aiming at, my advice is to investigate what legal entities are available for you as a startup in the jurisdiction you intend to either operate, sell, or receive the investment in.

In Croatia, most startups choose a limited liability company (Cro. *društvo sa ograničenom odgovornošću*, or DOO). This is the most common legal entity, and it enables them to have as many founders/directors as they wish and to operate freely. A DOO is also the most common form for any Croatian company, and laws and regulations are written to address them, so there exists a high level of certainty when it comes to operational and statutory issues.

A DOO is also relatively easy to incorporate and easy to liquidate. The greatest challenge with a DOO is that its equity structure and share issuance are not as smooth as one can find in joint stock companies (Cro. *dioničko društvo*, or DD) or limited liability companies in the UK/US. Generally, in Eastern European countries, even if it's called an LLC, it's *definitely* not the same LLC as in more advanced economies.

The Croatian company articles of incorporation (Cro. *društveni ugovor*) define equity through share capital, but you are limited by the amount and structure of the share capital and cannot issue additional shares unless you increase the share capital amount.

You are also restricted by law in the minimum amount such share capital can be nominated (€10) and also by the rule that any share capital amount has to be rounded to the same amount (For example, you cannot have a share valued at €45, it has to be either €40 or €50).

CHAPTER 2 GUEST CHAPTER: A FOUNDER'S GUIDE THROUGH THE LEGAL JUNGLE

This brings headaches to the founders and investors in any investment round where the percentage that is commonly spoken of when any investment is mentioned cannot be accurately reflected in the shareholder book. Luckily, shares can be structured and designed so they meet legal criteria and investment goals. Usually, the nominal value of shares is transferred, and any remaining amount is paid directly to the capital reserves of the company DOO.

I mentioned the DD type of company above, and now is a convenient time to mention why a DD as a legal form in Croatia is not a good idea. A DOO has a legal requirement for €2500 minimum share capital, and it may even be as low as €1 if you go for a form called a "simple DOO" (Cro. *jednostavno društvo sa ograničenom odgovornošću*). For a DD, you need a minimum amount of €25,000, and there are many more requirements when it comes to organizational structure (general assembly, supervisory board, management board), decision making, and more legal requirements to attend to than with a DOO. A DOO has only a management board (one or more directors) that operationally leads the company and shareholders meet only when there is a business need to do so.

In startups, the founders are usually the only shareholders and directors in the company, and they can make use of the flexible modes of management and structure, which makes DOOs more suitable for their purpose than DDs.

Beware that any transfer of DOO shares (Cro. *poslovni udjel*) must be in notarial form and tax authorities have to be notified about such transfers.

The notarial fee is calculated on the nominal value of the shares being transferred/share capital amount, and this is one of the reasons transactions are usually structured so that most of the investment is paid through capital reserves and not by an increase of share capital.

Do not forget that tax on share transfer exists in Croatia.

Finally, one more form of business has been rather popular in Croatia lately is the so-called *paušalni obrt* (often translated as "sole proprietorship" or a "trade") but please avoid this mode of doing business as is not suitable for the equity structures, transfers, and investments that are expected in the startup world.

Paušalni obrt is great for freelancers—usually one-person bands that have few clients and offer products/services irregularly, with a constant flow of new clients. For those needs it's preferable to the DOO because of easier bookkeeping and favorable tax treatment. No VC will ever invest in this type of business because it is simply not designed to support equity structures.

How to Take Investments

Ideally, you will not have even embarked on the startup journey before finding a customer (or a rich uncle) who will finance your early development, but that's often not how it goes. Once you are done with all of your life savings, have burned your family money, and even your friends have nothing more to lend you, but you have managed to develop an MVP or have hit the perfect market fit, you are ready for investments.

In the initial pre-seed round, apart from FFF (fools, friends, and family), you can also count on angel investors and different sorts of free money. However, beware: all grants come with strings attached, such as through reporting criteria that might prove to be rather time-consuming and compulsory attendance at workshops or different events hosted by the grant giver.

When choosing an angel investor, the crucial thing is to build a long-term relationship on safe and sound grounds of mutual trust and values. Try to choose "smart money" in all stages of funding—money that comes with experience, advice, guidance, and a great network that will stick with you in both good and hard times.

CHAPTER 2 GUEST CHAPTER: A FOUNDER'S GUIDE THROUGH THE LEGAL JUNGLE

Having said that, the usual method to get funded by angel investors in the last few years in Croatia has been through convertible loan agreements/notes (CLN). In a nutshell, this is an agreement between the founders, company, and angel investors whereby the loan is granted to the company for a specific agreed purpose with the possibility to convert the value of the loan to a certain percentage of the equity in your company.

Even if you skip the angel investing stage and hop into the venture or corporate investment stage, you will be presented with the same initial document called a term sheet. The term sheet is a minimum requirement agreement on the conditions of the investment to be received and to be agreed in detail either in CLN or in an investment agreement.

Before being offered a term sheet, the investor will demand that you and your company go through a due diligence process to establish the status of your startup. Depending on the findings of the due diligence, you will be offered a term sheet for future investment.

My strong recommendation is to enter the due diligence process with a spirit of cooperation and transparency for both parties. It is a small test of your future relationship.

The basic components of any term sheet are

- The investment amount
- Duration of the investment
- Percentage of equity taken
- Condition for (semi)exit and/or conversion of loan into equity
- Details on future investment rounds (so-called qualified financings)
- Any special arrangements such as liquidation preference (treatment such seed investors get in case liquidation of the company occurs)

CHAPTER 2 GUEST CHAPTER: A FOUNDER'S GUIDE THROUGH THE LEGAL JUNGLE

The standard term sheet wording is rather strict and incomprehensible to the average founder, so do find a lawyer who specializes in startups or corporate law in general. Ask questions, and when in doubt, add wording (schedules) to your investment agreement, providing examples of any scenarios you have talked about.

Such schedules enable you to play together with scenarios and to determine the mode for resolving future issues. Moreover, they establish clear wording on the true wills and intentions of all parties involved.

When drafted, CLNs and/or investment agreements will and must include details and clauses agreed in the term sheet. Usually, the term sheet itself is not binding between the parties, apart from its confidentiality clause, and only the final CLN and/or investment agreement creates obligations between signatories.

After the term sheet is agreed upon by all sides, it's time to start making it happen. The actual relations between you as cofounders and investors must be determined further, not only in the investment agreement but also in the articles of association (AOA) (Cro. *društveni ugovor*) for your company.

It is also typical to have a minimum/template AOA to be filled with the company register and disclosed to any third party, and a separate shareholder agreement (SA) whereby more detailed and confidential parts of your agreement are written.

AOA is the document where you set so-called *leaving clauses* of *tag along* (when a third party offers to buy the equity from other shareholders) or *drag along* (when you are offered purchase and you drag other shareholder's shares to the joint sale).

Also, there are usually clauses of first refusal rights or pre-emption rights that enable the remaining shareholders to acquire a share of the leaving shareholder first, under certain agreed terms.

CHAPTER 2   GUEST CHAPTER: A FOUNDER'S GUIDE THROUGH THE LEGAL JUNGLE

All the above-listed considerations, and many more, have to be considered by founders at the moment they seek and receive investment, and my advice is to hire professional support and consult with other shareholders who have experience with earlier investments and more mature startups.

> **PERSONAL EXAMPLE: A QUARREL BETWEEN FOUNDERS DESTROYS A COMPANY**
>
> Even the best friendships can fall apart when people find themselves in unfamiliar situations. In my mentorship experience, it's easy to find startups founded by best friends who did not make a contract that spells out what happens if one of the founders wants out.
>
> In one such case, the founder who was leaving held the belief that it is absolutely right for him to hold a significant amount of company equity even if he would not be contributing to the company, which the other founder disputed. Without a contract, this quarrel was not resolved, the toxicity spilled out into the company's daily operations, and it eventually led to the company's premature closure.
>
> No one needs a contract when things are going well. Contracts are there to govern what happens when something goes wrong.

CHAPTER 3

Setting Goals

TL;DR

- You don't have to know the future, but having a plan helps you create it.

- Different people (including founders!) have different definitions of success. Be aware of those differences.

- Be aware of terminology. What is an MVP, and what is the difference between incubators and accelerators?

- Immediately start looking for clients and investors abroad.

What's Not a Startup?

Anything with "agency" in its name is not a startup. Agencies can be very good businesses. There's nothing wrong with them. But they scale by hiring people instead of buying hardware, and investors don't like that because people are more expensive than hardware. Car mechanic shops are not good startups. You would need to open thousands of locations globally to reach a startup-like spread. But they can be good franchises. So can bakeries.

CHAPTER 3   SETTING GOALS

Startups are just one form of business, with relatively set rules. Nothing is preventing you from calling any kind of a young business endeavor a "startup" but be prepared that people will disagree with you.

Small businesses that don't grow and expand rapidly are usually called *lifestyle businesses*. Everything from a dentist or attorney's office to a bakery or a shoemaker shop is a lifestyle business and can provide you with a satisfying and challenging business for the rest of your life. Startups are insanely hard.

What's a Stealth-Mode Startup?

Usually a scam. Howard H. Aiken, one of IBM's earliest engineers, said, "Don't worry about people stealing your ideas. If your ideas are any good, you'll have to ram them down people's throats."

Meaning: A good, original idea, going into a blue ocean market (a *blue ocean market* is one *without* much competition; read *Blue Ocean Strategy* by W. Chan Kim and Renee Mauborgne[1]) is an idea that few people currently think is interesting, because if a lot of people thought it was interesting, everyone would be doing it.

Specifically, you should never worry about sharing your ideas and progress at startup-oriented events, conferences, pitching competitions, and such because everyone there is too busy pitching their own ideas to give your idea any attention. And even if they did, the biggest part of an idea is its execution. If a couple of random guys from a conference who hear about your idea for five minutes can take it and make a better business out of it than you (who's been thinking about it for years) can, then maybe your idea is not that good.

Remember, the low-hanging fruit has already been picked.

---

[1] W. Chan Kim & Renee Mauborgne, *Blue Ocean Strategy: How to Create Uncontested Market Space and Make the Competition Irrelevant* (Brighton, MA: Harvard Business Review Press, 2015)

As for VCs and other investors, they are too busy counting money to be involved with something as distasteful as actual hard work. Besides, why get involved in forming new teams to implement ideas when they have free labor at their disposal (namely you) to do it for them? If the idea is good, they'll profit in any case, so why complicate things?

I am not saying there are no bad actors and copying doesn't happen. There certainly are companies dedicated to copying/reimplementing ideas which seem to attract interest, but wasting your time worrying about that is beyond counterproductive if you can instead work on making and (more importantly) selling your product as far and wide as you can. Brand recognition, if you can establish it, in a wide market area, is the surest way to make copycats irrelevant.

What Do Startups Do?

Firstly, let's discuss what businesses in general do. They create value for their customers and for themselves. This is not trivial to accomplish. It's difficult to find something to do that results in value both for you and for your customers.

It's much easier to do it one-sided, but that's not a successful business. For example, you might create a product that is lovely to use and gets high marks from potential users, but they simply don't want to pay for it. That kind of product probably creates value for the customers, but not for the company.

As a creative person, you surely have a lot of ideas for products that seem good, and you consider them promising because you and the people you know would use such products. But will they pay for them? If you're creating a meeting/dating service for cat lovers and dog haters, the intended audience will probably love it, but will they pay for it? If not them, who will?

CHAPTER 3   SETTING GOALS

You may be leaning towards placing ads on your web/app for earning money, but please do not focus on that. "Scaling" by earning money from advertising is not a good startup strategy, unless you are creating a software platform that manages advertising itself on a global scale, like Google did.

In short, what you think doesn't matter. You really need to go out there and ask people if they will use the thing you want to create and how much they will pay for it. You might find out that yes, they want it, and yes, they will pay for it, but the amount is too small for the business to succeed. But if you don't ask, you will never know.

Do not hire third-party agencies and services to do market research for you as an early-stage startup. They need to make money too, and they are a service business, so they don't want to spend much time on a small client like yourself. You are the founder; the buck stops with you, and you need to invest the time (often huge amounts of time!) in doing the research. I warmly recommend reading *The Mom Test* by Rob Fitzpatrick[2].

Everyone Wants Recurring Revenue

This is directly related to why agency businesses are almost never considered startups. Investors, like most of the human species, want money for nothing and their chicks for free (to borrow from Dire Straits). In today's world, that means achieving recurring revenue, mostly through subscriptions for a SaaS product.

There are many examples where startups shoe-horned the subscription business model into what they are doing, just to extract that recurring money and make investors happy. Honestly, it's hard to fault them. Without naming names, here are some examples of businesses that did that:

---

[2] Rob Fitzpatrick, *The Mom Test: How to Talk to Customers & Learn if Your Business is a Good Idea When Everyone is Lying to You* (CreateSpace Independent Publishing Platform, 2013).

- A company that produces a very specific version of a tablet computer locked in their customers to paying monthly subscription for backing up their content.

- A company that has a legal document template business, with a nice web wizard that guides you with yes-or-no questions, makes you pay monthly for their service even if you never need to change those documents once they are created and can download & host them yourself.

- A company that sells security cameras charges you a monthly subscription if you want to extract videos and images from the camera in any way online, even if you do it manually.

- Twitter toys around with charging a monthly fee just for showing a blue mark next to your username, without added value. It's like a "hat" in games.

- Computer games started charging "season ticket" subscriptions to get new content (DLCs).

- A (failed) company producing a juice maker made the subscription "hidden" by forcing you to buy only their fruit and vegetables in special bags.

- A big producer of graphics and video editing desktop software stopped selling that software as-seen and started selling monthly access licenses.

While it is very possible to build a successful business where you sell something to a client once and then optionally charge them maintenance fees, that's somehow considered less monetizable (or with a less predictable cash flow) than forcing a subscription model.

CHAPTER 3   SETTING GOALS

Again, it is up to you as a founder to decide if this is something you want to implement.

What's a Successful Startup?

Success comes in many forms, ranging from "leaving my mark on the world" to "gathering enough money to work on the next idea" to "making my father proud."

Notice that "making money and retiring" isn't on the list, and that's for a couple of reasons:

- If you have the urge and the skills to earn enough money with a startup, you'll be bored to death if you quit and actually try to retire.
- It turns out that money itself is a much, much, *much* weaker motivator than any of the examples stated above.

Personally, I'm in the "make enough money to work on the next idea" camp.

In almost all startups, the founders eventually decide they're successful enough (or have had enough) and pull back from the front lines, or even make an exit (i.e., sell their shares in the company). For them, that's likely the point at which they consider the whole endeavor a success.

Very specifically and to the point: a startup is *not* a success when it has received an investment. This deserves to be stated again in a different way: investment money is *not* what constitutes success. What can be an *indicator of potential success* is the fact that the investment happened at all, because it shows that the investor, as a reasonably neutral third party, thinks you are doing a good job and expects you will continue doing so for the foreseeable future.

For shareholders, the criterion for success is less inspiring but more concrete: it's all about the money they will receive either through an exit of their own (i.e., selling their share of the company to someone else) or through dividends. In most cases, they should be prepared to wait at least three to five years before they see success.

One of the ideas floating around is that a successful startup is specifically created and optimized for a particular outcome, and that's usually to be bought by a larger company after a set number of years. Not every startup should do that, and for most, the future's not set at the start.

If you're going to follow this idea, you should go all in. Create a detailed persona of your buyer company before you even start. What kind of company is it (with real-world examples)? Why would it buy your company (or what should your company become to be bought by it)? Has it bought similar startups before? At what valuation would you sell?

In truth, the majority of startups are indeed more or less quietly bought by bigger companies. You probably know the statistic that 95% of all startups fail, but if even 5% of them succeed, where are they? If you can name 50 successful worldwide startups, you've done your homework well, but that still leaves thousands of them each year that are successful but not talked about as much as the superstars are. Most of them are simply sold to big players without raising attention.

Investors, especially VC funds, love when you talk about exit plans. They themselves are only buying shares in your company to sell them later at a higher price, so they want to hear from you who that buyer could be as soon as possible.

If your desired outcome is an IPO, few early investors will believe you, especially in Europe. But if it's "being bought by Microsoft," that sounds a lot better.

CHAPTER 3   SETTING GOALS

Staying Afloat

A person I greatly admire told me early in my startup journey that staying afloat (i.e., keeping the company existing) is a matter of "founder magic." As a founder, you will probably do a lot of things you never thought you'd be capable of doing, just to keep your baby from sinking.

- **Solvency** is the term used to describe a company's capability to meet its long-term financial obligations. Another way of looking at it is that a solvent business is one that has positive net worth: the total assets are more than the total liabilities. It means it can pay back its loans, taxes, and non-optional expenses such as accountancy services.

- **Liquidity** is the term used to describe that the company has more than zero cash in its bank account and can satisfy its short-term debts, such as paying employees' salaries, cloud services, software licenses, or office space rent.

How you achieve both is indeed magic, especially in the early days (which could last years). You could go into debt, you could charm more angel investors, you could win a lottery, you could creatively schedule outgoing payments . . . it doesn't matter, as long as the company is staying afloat.

When Does a Startup Stop Being a Startup?

This question has several, pretty fuzzy and subjective answers, but as a general checklist, here are the events which will probably result in people not calling you a startup anymore:

- The company raises a Series A round.
- The company is bought by another company.
- The company closes down.
- More than five years have passed since its founding.

The last scenario is the most difficult one. What next? You don't have a startup, but you do have a company that has survived for five+ years. Is it a good company? Is it worth sticking around with it? Are you comfortable with having VCs in the company's ownership or debt structure, so they claim rights on profits/dividends? You're the only one who can answer these questions.

What you probably will not and even cannot do is close down the company and start another one doing the same business. Usually, VCs will have a clause in your contract penalizing that.

How to Approach the Market

One difference between the US and Europe is in how companies approach and address their potential customers in marketing styles. The US style is often perceived to be direct, assertive, and pushy from the point of view of Europe, and in extreme circumstances can sometimes be called "uncultured." However, it works, and it works better than the shy and somber style often associated with Europe.

In the B2B context, the European style is often to timidly present your product at trade shows, conferences, or even pitching events and wait for interested people to approach you. The older generation (of potential clients and partners) often state that they do not want to hear direct business proposals from people they don't already trust. But despite that, or even because of that, sometimes pushing your product assertively actually works better in most cases; sometimes you have the opportunity to surprise them with your expediency.

CHAPTER 3   SETTING GOALS

The Lifecycle of a VC-Backed Company

Skip this section if you have money.

For the rest of us, the journey of creating a successful startup will go through some common phases. Each of those phases corresponds to a certain type of money-gathering activity that works at that phase and has some conventional expectations. I present them in the following table:

Phase name	Description	Investment source	Expected outcome
Idea	You only have a PowerPoint slide deck and a gleam in your eye.	Friends, fools, and family (FFF), possibly angel investors	Make a PowerPoint deck that won't make an accountant weep.
Proof of concept	You cobble together something that looks like it may be useful to someone. It doesn't have to contain the entirety of your master plan.	Angel investors, incubators	Get feedback on the proof of concept from FFF and potential clients, then iterate and refine it. Charm an investor.
Minimum viable product (MVP)	You've made something which can actually be used by a human being who isn't you, and they find it useful.	Accelerators, maybe even early customers if you are lucky	Get a couple of early paying clients. Refine the MVP through feedback from them. Probably the right time to establish a company and think of hiring.

(continued)

Phase name	Description	Investment source	Expected outcome
Beta product version	Something you are not constantly ashamed of is being used daily by your client(s).	Accelerators, seed (early stage) VCs	Prove that you are capable of selling it in a volume that makes money, which could be interesting to VCs.
Version 1.0	You are transitioning from a startup to a scaleup. There is no doubt people want your product and that you are capable of both making and selling it. The question is, how much can you earn?	Series A VCs — probably the first "serious" investors	Grab a significant market share in a non-trivial niche. Make money.

This table deliberately omits a column titled "investment amount" because that varies madly. What amount you can attract at which stage depends on how good you are at persuading investors to invest in you, and on plain old luck. As a rule of thumb, never accept a "seed" round lower than €300,000 (lower amounts are the province of angel investors and incubators), or a series A round that isn't in the millions. See Chapter 5 for a discussion on the startup financial lifecycle.

Do not be afraid of shopping around for more money. Do not get discouraged if you pitch to hundreds of potential investors at each stage. Do not think you have enough money and can finally stop raising more.

CHAPTER 3   SETTING GOALS

On Hedging

It would be best if I could answer this topic with simply "Don't," but life isn't simple.

The term "hedging" in this context means running multiple companies/operations/projects/activities to minimize the risk of one of them failing. Colloquially, it could also mean running multiple operations even if risk is not a concern, just because you feel you can do it, or it seems like a good opportunity. Having a "day job" and founding a startup in parallel is also considered "hedging," even if you are not doing it to mitigate risk but to earn money to bootstrap the business.

Generally, hedging always means splitting your attention, and when that happens you will almost always miss something crucial at the time you can least afford to make such a mistake.

For most people, whether to hedge or not will depend on the stage of life they are in. Unless you are independently wealthy, the advisability of hedging could be summarized as

- **If you're in your twenties**: ALWAYS GO ALL IN; don't hedge. Pick something you can be passionate about for five to ten years, and just do it. Continue doing it if it makes sense. Live in your parents' basement, or in a car, or a dormitory, and just dedicate your time to the business you want to create.

- **If you're in your sixties**: ALWAYS HEDGE, since if you fail, you most likely don't have the time to recover before your living standard drops significantly, and you probably don't have the social network or safety nets to support you if you fail. Many of your affluent friends you met when younger might be dead already.

For the rest of us, it's somewhere in between.

CHAPTER 3   SETTING GOALS

Who Buys European Startups?

Not European companies, that's for sure[3].

Just the idea that a European company would buy WhatsApp, a company with 30-ish employees, for $16 billion seems ridiculous. That's a surprising fact in itself, since judging purely by the numbers, Europe has many more large companies than the US. The US has a huge advantage (about three times) in the number of small companies, while Europe seems to have optimized itself to have a few large ones (source: OECD).

About 75% of EU startups were bought by US companies, mostly from the Silicon Valley[4].

This is slowly changing, though, as there is a new generation of big companies with international reputations that have themselves grown through the VC path (did you know Spotify is a Swedish company?) and will act as M&A instigators in the future.

Only 24% of European startups that get bought are bought by companies outside the US and the EU[5].

PERSONAL EXAMPLE: IGNORE STEALTH-MODE STARTUPS

About 6 months after my startup was founded, I read an article which told a vague story of an up-and-coming startup in the exact niche I was aiming at, but without details. The startup was labelled as a "stealth startup" with a couple of clues thrown here and there about what it was aiming to do, and an

---

[3] Emerald.com, *Journal of Business Strategy*, Alessia Pisoni and Alberto Onetti, "When startups exit: comparing strategies in Europe and the USA," www.emerald.com/insight/content/doi/10.1108/JBS-02-2017-0022/full/html?skipTracking=true

[4] Source "State of European Tech": https://startupeuropepartnership.eu/3-4-startups-acquiredus-companies/

[5] Source "State of European Tech": https://stateofeuropeantech.com/1.european-teach-a-new-reality

CHAPTER 3   SETTING GOALS

information that they've quickly raised tens of millions of USD in funding. I admit I got scared. Will their product be revolutionary? Will it make our product obsolete? They certainly had the money. But now, a couple of years down the line, and the company is hardly seen anywhere, and my startup still exists.

There's no use in being scared of competition, especially of stealth mode startups. If they were any good, they'd be out with a product much sooner than they advertise.

CHAPTER 4

Guest Chapter: On the Franchise Model for Startups

By Andrija Andy Čolak

TL;DR

- Most franchises are leveraging the geographical distribution of a particular business concept to spread faster and easier.
- Even startups can make use of the franchise model.
- Similar to other types of investors, you must have solid proof the business can succeed before you become attractive to potential franchisees.
- Franchises can have many interesting streams of revenue.

I am the owner of one of the earliest and most successful franchises in Croatia, Surf'n'Fries, and I have given a lot of thought to how to start, manage, and profit from a franchise business model. I'm currently also operating as a consultant in my own company, Colak Franchise Consulting Group.

CHAPTER 4   GUEST CHAPTER: ON THE FRANCHISE MODEL FOR STARTUPS

The franchise business model has only recently arrived on the Eastern European markets where we are located. Consequently, not many people understand the potential for scaling offered by this business model. In this part of the world, franchises are still very much assumed to be about fast food, but that's clearly wrong.

The franchise model is beginning to be applied in multiple industries, including IT, through so-called digital franchise scaling for apps. Lately, apps like "Send me a trainer" are spreading in hyper speed throughout global markets using a franchise model. Their offer is a concession on using and managing an app in a certain geographic area.

Even if mega corporations like Amazon are not directly investing in this model, they operate certain parts of their business like a franchise, such as last-mile deliveries. This model certainly has a large role in the 21st century because it's inherently based on a win-win principle, which is a key element for a sustainable and successful business.

Why Franchise Your Concept

"Why don't you open your own stores? Why bother with that franchise thing? Doesn't that make others earn the money you could have been earning?" I've often heard these questions. These questions are often asked by those with a narrow view of business and who are not open to new ways of doing things.

Indeed, we are all interested in profits, but there are many ways to get them. Equally important is that we create opportunities which advance the industry, or a region.

The franchise business model provides a win-win relationship between business partners. We all have our own skills, preferences, and blind spots. There are some entrepreneurs who excel in creating new concepts and new products and putting them on the market, and there are those who are best at pulling out every cent from a business, if given a strong concept.

CHAPTER 4   GUEST CHAPTER: ON THE FRANCHISE MODEL FOR STARTUPS

Franchises play well to those strengths. Someone creates a strong concept and proves it in the market, some invest capital, some invest labor, and everyone profits. The brand grows in strength and reach.

Specifically, I can think of three main reasons why converting your concept or brand into a franchise is a good idea:

1. **It is much less capital intensive to grow globally.**

    In a franchise business, the franchisee (the person or business that has acquired the rights to operate under a franchise license) is the one investing capital in setting up a new shop or office. In addition, they are also paying for the license. This means that the franchisor (the company that has created the franchise and is licensing it) with a scalable and proven concept can, in theory, have thousands of shops or offices globally without directly investing in any of them. This can be hugely beneficial compared to financing them directly.

2. **The benefits of franchisee vs. manager**

    Who will be more involved and have more skin in the game: a manager you hired to lead a remote office, or a franchisee who has invested their own money and time into establishing a business? Of course the franchisee is the better choice here. Some studies have shown up to 30% better performance between franchisees and salaried managers, when operating under an identical concept, and it boils down to having skin in the game.

    Of course, your skill in picking up franchisees (because you want to pick ones that will advance your brand and business goals) will play a role in your overall success. Think of it this way: finding a good franchisee is killing two birds with one stone. They are an investor who doesn't require equity in your business, and they are a business partner who doesn't require additional motivation, while also working harder than a run-of-the-mill employee.

3. **The local network and local market knowledge**

    It's difficult to take your business beyond the limits of your starting city, and it gets harder the farther you go. What do you know about what's going on and who's doing what in another state or continent? You don't know anyone there, and maybe you don't speak the language and know nothing about their laws and customs.

With a franchise approach, all this becomes easier as you rely on the franchisee to be your source of local knowledge and a solver of problems you wouldn't know how to deal with. This makes them a very valuable asset to which you otherwise either wouldn't have access to or would spend a lot of money and time trying to obtain. They are there to relieve you of the burden of establishing a local company; scouting, buying, or leasing a location; finding workers; and other operational things in a remote area.

Other Reasons

Other than the three reasons above, there are of course others: a franchise operation can be a stable source of income through licensing fees, there's an opportunity for product improvement through feedback coming from a diverse set of franchisees, and it's an opportunity to network globally.

CHAPTER 4   GUEST CHAPTER: ON THE FRANCHISE MODEL FOR STARTUPS

Four Steps to a Successful Franchise
Step 1: Create Something Successful, Profitable, and Scalable

My own story begins in 2009 when we created the Surf'n'Fries brand and opened the first shop in Rijeka, Croatia. It was a small shop (27 m2), and it was in a bad location. We made a lot of early mistakes, but we persevered and grew from there into Croatia's most spread franchise business, operating in 20 countries all over the world, with a revenue of $5 million yearly. And that's with French fries and dressings, in a country that is a tourist magnet.

The conventional wisdom here was to just do what everyone else did and establish our own shops, go into debt to finance them, or enter into shady business partnerships to get access to the best locations on the coast. Luckily, we had no idea what we were doing because we now realize that going the conventional route would have been disastrous for us.

Our brand (S'n'F for short) was, and is, very different from the norm. It only sells French fries, it operates under a foreign name (this is Croatia, remember?), the interior looks more like a fashion boutique than a fast food place, it has fancy custom-made packaging. It's like the Apple Store of fast foods; everything screams high-end branding.

We did alright. But, as always in business, while being different is an important factor, it's much more important to be profitable because that leads to opening more franchises.

In our case, the differentiation was the selling factor, but at the time we still didn't know we were going to do a franchise. This one small shop was doing 1000 portions a day, and we thought that was a lot. I thought I had to repeat this success somehow, but the next problem was how to optimally use the resulting capital to grow. Was establishing another shop really the best answer?

CHAPTER 4   GUEST CHAPTER: ON THE FRANCHISE MODEL FOR STARTUPS

Step 2: Make It Desirable (to Entrepreneurs)

Monkey see, monkey do. If there's a runaway success in the market, others will want to be a part of it.

We had the good fortune to have direct experience the very same year we opened, with people coming to our shop and asking for guidelines on how to open a similar business. Even so, it didn't yet occur to us to sell them a franchise. Instead, we helped them with advice as best we could, and continued scratching our heads in search of an answer on how to grow our little shop. Eventually, it dawned on us that we were staring an opportunity of a lifetime, and at the same time we could turn competitors into business partners!

As we had no experience in franchises, we started learning. We ordered books from Amazon and went to work. Our first franchise shop was opened in Zagreb the very same year, and then it spread to other towns and eventually abroad.

My key point here is that we went into franchising at the correct time: when we had a successful shop that not only had good turnover, but also a clear indication that other people wanted to run a similar business. People needed to see they could make a profit from it, too.

Step 3: Work with an Expert Who Will Set Up Your Franchise Model

We started on our own, without expertise, and we managed the best we could, making mistakes along the way. The situation back then was bleak. There was no one to ask for advice in this part of Europe, and hardly anyone had experience with the franchise concept, let alone the business model.

Consequently, our first attempt was wrong in many aspects. We gave the franchisee almost everything and asked almost nothing in return, which placed us in a vulnerable position. Our books of standards were

CHAPTER 4   GUEST CHAPTER: ON THE FRANCHISE MODEL FOR STARTUPS

too short and lacked important points, and we didn't even write our operations manual. We just didn't know how important they were, and truth be told, we didn't have a clear picture of how to write them even if we wanted to.

We paid a substantial price because those things are the fundamentals, and we were lacking in them. Some of the consequences were that our franchisees had too much freedom to tweak our concept in a direction we didn't want it to go, and others asked to change our deal. Some early franchisees failed.

To help others learn from my mistakes and the things I've learned, I've established the CFCG Group consultancy business. Of course, you don't have to go with us, but do try to find someone to consult with on your franchise journey. The more experienced, the better. This person or team will help you with all the things that influence the success of your franchise, ranging from the business model to various paperwork to franchise-specific documents such as the book of standards and the operations manual.

There's a lot of bad advice floating around when it comes to franchises. For the last ten years, I've encountered many businesses that were set up very poorly, and that includes both beginners and, surprisingly, established franchises. I've even encountered established (but young) franchises that were internally set up so poorly that the only advice I could give them was to start from scratch.

We started badly and were lucky to succeed up to the point that we did. Some businesses tried to copy us, including our mistakes, and failed miserably. My advice to you is to find someone based on their experience and past references. Their cost will be worth it when your business succeeds. Don't try to do everything yourself. The opportunity cost of the wasted time is too big to ignore.

CHAPTER 4   GUEST CHAPTER: ON THE FRANCHISE MODEL FOR STARTUPS

Step 4: Start Saying "No" As Quickly As Possible

One of the worst things you can experience as a franchise owner is to see your franchises fail. Not only emotionally, as you've lost business partners or territory, but also financially. One of the criterion that prospective franchisees look for is the ratio of successful to failed franchises. Failed franchises are literally preventing you from attaining new franchisees. The reverse also holds: a track record of successful franchises will easily attract new franchisees.

The key takeaway is to develop a keen sense of balance between driving growth by accepting anyone for a franchisee and keeping an eye on quality.

What Are the Revenue Streams in a Franchise?

I'm happy to say that we have a substantial volume of inquiries for franchising different brands and concepts, which is a good sign for franchises in general in this part of the world. One of the most often discussed topics, understandably, is about profit generation streams available to franchisors.

1. **Entry fee**

    Entry fees are paid once per unit of the franchise, for the duration of the contract. For a new franchisee, this fee is paid at the beginning of the business relationship between the franchisor and the franchisee, and for existing franchisees, each time a new franchise unit is opened or a contract is renewed.

CHAPTER 4 GUEST CHAPTER: ON THE FRANCHISE MODEL FOR STARTUPS

Franchise contracts usually last a fixed number of years, let's say ten years, and the entry fee is a part of what gives the franchisee rights to exploit the franchise for the duration of the contract.

Entry fees exist to encourage commitment and show of faith on behalf of the franchisee to stick with the deal. Usually, those who wish to find a way to avoid the entry fee are not the ones you want to do business with.

2. **Royalty fee**

Royalty fees are paid regularly from the franchisee to the franchisor and are calculated as a part of the revenue (not profit), usually between 4% and 7%. This fee is usually paid annually.

For example, if the franchise makes €100,000 in revenue in a particular year and the contract is for a yearly royalty fee of 7%, the franchisor will receive €7000 (after taxes), depending on the contract, for that year. This fee is paid continually, year on year, for the duration of the contract.

3. **Marketing fee**

The marketing fee is sometimes paid by the franchisees to the common marketing fund managed by the franchisor. This fee is usually set between 1% and 3%. To avoid misunderstandings, the franchisor should take care to be as transparent as possible with this fund and to follow all best practices for this kind of relationship. The franchisees should know when and where is their money spent.

4. **Markup/kickback scheme**

   The franchisor could have separate deals with providers of certain goods or services used in the usual operations of the franchises and earn additional profit from them. For example, the franchisor could regulate that only certain products or brands can be used in a part of a franchise's operation, to ensure the quality of the final products, and have a deal with those brands for a kickback fee. If a franchisee with €100,000 in yearly revenue operates with a direct cost (COGS) of 35% and buys everything from a specific business that has a kickback agreement with the franchisor, the franchisor earns an extra €1750 yearly. (100,000 * 0.35 = 25,000; 25,000 * 0.07 = 1750).

A Summary Example

I love to learn through examples, so here is an example of a franchise business that has all of the fees discussed above.

- Assuming the franchise generates €100,000 in revenue (to simplify calculations)
- Assuming the franchise opens two new locations/offices a year
- With an entry fee of €10,000
- With a royalty fee of 6%
- With a marketing fee of 1%
- With a kickback scheme of 7% over 35% of purchased goods

The franchisor's yearly income for the first year could be

- €20,000 from entry fees
- €12,000 from royalty fees
- €2000 from marketing fees
- €4900 from the kickback scheme
- In total: €38,900

The €100,000 figure I am working with here is just to simplify my calculations. Many F&B and retail industry products will dwarf this income. Also, it's common to open more than two new locations/offices yearly. Sometimes there may be hundreds of them, depending on the simplicity and demand. There's also the possibility of franchising the franchise itself, having "master franchise" agreements with businesses whose goal is to develop individual franchises in a certain geographical area, such as a state or a continent, and those agreements can have a similar fee structure.

When Does a Franchise Become Interesting to Investors and Potential Buyers?

What creates value in franchises? What are investors or buyers looking for when they are shopping for a franchise?

After more than a decade in franchises, I learned from my own chain as it grew from a small shop into an international chain, but also by studying others who have succeeded. Many company owners work tirelessly day by day to increase their businesses' value so they can achieve a substantial "exit" (i.e., sell the company). No matter what product or company they are developing, they often get blindsided and miss the opportunities to build a scalable system that could do much of their work for them.

CHAPTER 4 GUEST CHAPTER: ON THE FRANCHISE MODEL FOR STARTUPS

The importance of scalability cannot be understated. All VC and PE funds are searching for concepts where scalability is the primary indicator their investment will yield a multiple in returns. If a concept isn't scalable, it basically means it will not achieve strong growth, and as such will most likely fail to entice both investors and buyers. Without scalability, all other components of a concept are most likely valueless.

The good news is that franchising a business or a concept puts an incredibly strong emphasis on scalability, and it can be applied to almost any industry. This is a mind shift for most people, as it switches them to think in terms of building systems that can be replicated multiple times, instead of just the single shop/small business. Speaking from experience, this kind of thinking is very much missing in Eastern Europe.

Most experts agree on these three basic characteristics the franchisors must possess:

1. **A proof of break-even**

    A franchise concept becomes interesting to potential franchisees when they can calculate how much time has to pass before they recover the entry fee for a single franchise unit and how long they need to work before they can also recover the (yearly) royalty fee.

    Having these numbers shows that the franchisor has a successful concept on their hands, one they can be reasonably certain can generate profit.

    Without them, it's mostly useless to pitch the concept to potential buyers/franchisees.. It's up to the franchisor to prove their concept is financially solid.

2. **Time**

    In general, the time spent developing and proving a concept cannot be shortened significantly, and the franchisor has to be ready for a multi-year process before their concept can take flight as a franchise. They need to do a lot of "debugging" of the concept, its operations, and branding before they can be sure it makes sense to offer it as a franchise, and that can cost a lot of money and time.

    This, of course, is not unique to franchises. Looking at regular startups, even the best funded ones with great teams and mentors need time to realize their vision.

3. **Productivity**

    I previously mentioned scalability as an integral part of the success equation, including investments and acquisitions. I will say it again: scalability is the primary reason why someone would want to buy your franchise or invest in your company.

    The road to there is thorny and long because proving a concept takes a lot of work, but after that, it becomes a little bit easier. Each new franchise unit yields more profit for the franchisor, but also benefits from all the past success and all the things they've learned so far. Processes get better, branding gets better, marketing gets better, and because of that, productivity rises.

It is especially beneficial if you can demonstrate that small increases in effort/cost can yield large productivity increases (exponential, even). If you can achieve that, you will have no problem attracting franchisees, partners, and investors.

Summary: Focus on Internal Processes First

As a franchisor, your primary duties are to prove a concept, and while doing that, to create and polish up its processes to perfection. It will take time, but that's normal. If you succeed, you will end up with a system that grows linearly in costs but exponentially in profitability. This is the point where everyone will want you.

Startups as Franchises

Though it's still not very common, there are examples of startups that operate as franchises. Usually, they are the ones that have figured out how to scale by opening some kind of offices or by establishing partnerships across wide geographic areas.

The example I've mentioned before, "Send me a Trainer" does this by franchising the handling of local demand for personal fitness trainers. It is also interesting because it is a digital franchise. In theory, the franchisee doesn't even have to have an office because the franchise provides online tools to manage trainers, their payrolls, clients, and schedules. The franchisee's job is basically to hire trainers and monitor their performance and customer satisfaction. It is also one of the more expensive franchises out there, with initial costs averaging €70,000. Their claim to fame, which is so far going strong since their founding in 2019 in a very rapidly growing industry, is that there ideally is very little for the franchisees to actually do.

CHAPTER 4   GUEST CHAPTER: ON THE FRANCHISE MODEL FOR STARTUPS

It's an interesting setup: this is an industry that clearly has a lot of hands-on contact with the clients and very much relies on the clients' satisfaction and their own reputation, which makes it difficult to operate fully online from a central location. It would be very difficult for them to be an "Uber for trainers" since, despite all their efforts, even Uber doesn't have as much control over the quality of their drivers as they would like to have.

In short, some local diligence is required. On the other hand, it would be very expensive for them to open proper offices across the globe, and the probability of finding an investor to finance that kind of expansion would be low. Instead, they made a franchise that kind of does both and neither at the same time and is considered a prosperous startup.

A key takeaway here is that the ideal case for a startup as a franchise is when that combination can solve the problem of global expansion by making use of local knowledge and presence.

PERSONAL EXAMPLE: DON'T SAY "YES" TO EVERY CLIENT

It took us several years with S'n'F and learning about franchise models to learn to say "no" to everyone who could damage our brand.

This is part of the experience. In early phases, franchises are often flattered that anyone has taken an interest and are highly motivated to spread. That leads them to accept bad deals such as bad locations and franchisees who are not familiar or completely ok with the concept or the brand, who will skimp on quality or workforce, or dozens of other things. In the short term, sure, you open a new franchise and it's very exciting, but it soon turns out that there's a big price to pay.

CHAPTER 5

Getting Money

TL;DR

- *Cheap money* is the money you can get without giving away equity.

- Investors are just people. Sometimes even they don't know what they want.

- It always pays to be socially charming. If you are not, learn to act it, or partner with a cofounder who is.

- Not all investors behave logically. Many do not care if your company succeeds individually.

- Do not spend time creating a product no one wants to buy or invest in. Discover this as early as possible, ideally before seeking money.

Equity and the Cap Table

Equity is often the most important thing you, as a founder, have in the company. Any loss of equity is expensive for your future prospects.

The capitalization table shows who owns what part of the company. It is an important document both for investors and for the distribution of profits. When the company is founded, only the founders are present in the cap table. When an investor makes an investment in exchange for equity, this is recorded in the cap table. The usual thing that happens when you distribute profits is that each entity in the cap table gets their proportional due, but this can be modified by other contracts.

Ways of Getting Money

The best way, bar none, of getting money is to sell something you have made (and can keep making cheaply). That something is called a product. If you don't have the product (yet), you need to acquire money some other way. There is a ladder of how "cheap" you can get the money you need, assuming the thing you value most is equity in your startup.

- **Grants:** Grants are free money. Some kind soul or organization will give your company money and will not require repayment of any significant kind. Grants frequently come with some conditions you must follow, though, such as limitations on what you can spend the money on, the reporting you must carry out, or some marketing activity you must perform to glorify the entity which bestowed their money on you.

- **Loans:** This one is also easy: a bank or a wealthy sheikh lends you money and expects to be paid back with interest in some way. This is still "cheap" in terms of not giving away any equity ownership to anyone but comes with an obligation to return the loaned amount plus interest in, usually, a very strictly defined timespan. Because of unpredictable nature of startup businesses, startups usually avoid loans because they cannot guarantee they will be successful enough in a fixed amount of time to pay them back.

- **Convertible loans:** These are loans that can either be paid back (plus interest) or get converted into equity. A particularly popular type of convertible loan in the US and the UK is the SAFE note. These are templated contracts that are pretty reasonable in what they offer and can be a very good deal for both you and your investors. Because of the templated nature of SAFE notes, they are also quick to implement, especially if the startup's HQ is in a business-friendly location (i.e., not Europe). Still, even in European bureaucracies, these are usually easy enough (though a good an experience lawyer will be needed to actually write the contract) to be an acceptable means of investment.

- **Equity:** The investor simply takes a certain percentage of the equity in exchange for hard cash. That's the negative. The positive is that you do not need to pay them anything back, as they have assumed the risk of co-owning the company with you, and in the early stages, they usually do not try to influence the running of the company or place any limits on what you can do with the money. They might have something to say about what happens if the company is dissolved or when it becomes a success.

The rule of thumb here is that you should give up as little equity as possible to gain as large an investment as possible. This is precisely the opposite of what investors want, so you should probably get lessons on haggling from an expert.

CHAPTER 5   GETTING MONEY

A Special Note about EU and Governmental Funds

The EU has proven to be willing to throw money around in the hope of empowering the startup ecosystems of its constituent countries, but the way this is done is often counterproductive. There are heavy restrictions and rules on how the money can be spent, and their definitions of what a good startup or a good general business is vary between hilariously funny and very naive. It seems that the people in charge think they can legislate businesses into being.

This has led to the proliferation of a new genre of literature: EU funding proposal fiction. Of course, if you can get a hold of a high-quality ghost-writer (a.k.a. an EU funding consultant) who can ride the waves of paperwork, and if you have enough bootstrap money to handle the "we'll only fund 50% of your proposal" type of grants, they might be a viable source of early (pre-seed) funding.

The EU has its own agenda and (often purely bean-counting) goals to achieve. Some requirements often seen in their funding projects' brochures that preclude early startups from making use of its funds are:

- That the startup has a minimum number of full-time employees—which is too much to ask for pre-revenue startups.

- That founders (or even a specific number of founders; I've seen a call where there had to be at least two founders) work full-time for the company—again, this can be too much to ask for a pre-revenue startup.

- The requirement that the funding is spent in a particular structure, such as: at most a certain percent on marketing, at most a certain percent on salaries —which is a silly restriction to impose on the highly dynamic environment of startups.

- That the company has to have a certain amount of cash reserves before they can apply, because the call will fund a proposal that is worth a certain minimum amount of money, and the company has to provide a certain percentage of it on its own.

- That the company protects its intellectual properties in any way possible. This is sometimes silly as there are no software patents in the EU, so in many cases the only things a startup can protect (i.e., use its meagre funds to pay for IP lawyers and patent office services) are name, design, and branding. But according to the EU, it *must* protect something if it's applying to most funding opportunities.

EU funding (but the same is often true for any kind of governmental funding) is sometimes fundamentally at odds with VC funding. While VCs like to see stories of a company earning revenue with a minimum number of employees (see how WhatsApp operated pre-acquisition) and will consider a high revenue-per-employee company much more attractive than its comparable competitors, the EU likes to see a lot of employees in a company, even if that means they are paid minimum wage because there's not enough cash for them to have decent salaries. The EU also likes to fund projects that have even a fictional positive impact on the society or the environment, and EU funding proposals often include such fiction just to increase their chances of being funded. It's just how the game is played. For example, the *UN sustainable development goals*[1] are currently popular.

---

[1] The United Nations, "*17 Goals*," https://sdgs.un.org/goals.

CHAPTER 5 GETTING MONEY

What Are Investors and What Do They Want?

Investors are mythical beings (until you get to know them) who, sometimes completely unfairly, are in possession of money you happen to urgently need.

It's as difficult to discuss what investors want as it is to discuss what individual people want. Of course, wants, needs, and communication are as messed up as with most people. They are only human, after all.

In theory, and this is what basically gets written on every investor's landing page, investors are seeking:

- A great team with bold ideas which will conquer the world.

- Proof the team can execute/deliver on their promise.

- Trust and great synergy between you and them.

In practice, you will soon discover that what the majority of investors who do not already have a relationship with you really want is more similar to the following list:

- That your product is something they themselves want to buy.

- That you charm them socially.

- That the bottom line looks good (i.e., they see you making a profit).

That's all ok in the honeymoon phase, but eventually, the vast majority of investors will only start looking at the bottom line and how they can extract value for themselves. This is normal and expected, as long as both sides know how to play the game.

If you happen to find an exception to this rule, it will probably be in the form of a mentor, and you *should not let them go*, no matter what. They will help you in more ways than just financially.

But let's focus on the official theory. Investors say they want to see competence, and they want you to demonstrate that they can trust you to execute your plan. Usually (unless it's a mentor situation), investors will punish you if you ask them to work with you on creating the plan. The story goes that it's your business, and they are only here for the ride.

The canonical way to satisfy that requirement is to show them that a) you've created something and b) that you have successfully sold something related to it, preferably many times over. Only inexperienced investors will require you to have a whole product ready when you come knocking at their door in the early stage, but you usually need to show them that you've sold something.

Do you know the story about the person who approached a top-level VC with nothing but an idea written on a napkin, and left the office with a $10 million seed round? Yeah, they either had five successful prior exits, or their dad was the fund manager; those are just about the only cases where you don't have to prove your ability before they give you money.

One mistake inexperienced founders make is to think they need to make and sell a crummy, half-baked, low-res version of the grand idea to demonstrate their ability. A much better choice is to create a highly polished single representative part that does something moderately useful by itself but obviously is a part of a bigger plan.

For example, if you are intent on making high-tech luxury fridges, the worst possible thing you can do as a proof of concept is to cobble up a n ugly but functional fridge in your garage, using components from your local DIY store, with uneven surfaces, rough edges, bad painting, thick insulation, a noisy cooler engine, held together by duct tape, and with some AliExpress-sourced blinkenlights stuck to it. Even if the whole thing works flawlessly, no one is going to be impressed and finance it.

A much better idea is just to create the box, without any active parts (so not a functional fridge). Make that box *look* perfect for the proof of concept and *feel* perfect for the MVP stage. Add dry ice to simulate cooling. Make it look like it should belong on a star ship, like its design was guided and approved by the ghost of Steve Jobs himself.

Sell the box. Not literally, but use the box to sign-on customers who will buy the finished fridge in the future when it's ready. Run a Kickstarter if you have to. Then ask investors for the money to develop the electronics and plumbing within (obviously, you are either an engineer yourself or have hired an engineer to verify the MVP box has enough room for the working parts).

The same goes for software. Suppose you have the idea of making an online platform for connecting cat lovers and dog haters together. What you should do first is a beautiful mini app with the most basic functionality required. Maybe you don't even need a database. Make the web app send you e-mails when someone signs up, and you will connect the lucky pairs manually by sending them introductory e-mails yourself, pretending to be a machine. You'll be the AI, the database, the web microservice, or even the blockchain.

If you can prove this scheme can make money, that's your MVP. Only after that will you raise an investment and hire someone competent enough to actually design a database and a recommendation system for you. Even if you have PhDs in both areas, you will be too busy running the company to do it yourself.

Types of Investors

Friends, fools, and family are your go-to investors when you have nothing but an idea. They might not even require written contracts from you, or to pay them back the money. Of course, you should do right by them and not weasel out of any obligations, because if you happen to succeed, you will need them even more than before for emotional support.

Angel investors are professional and semi-professional investors, usually just ordinary people who happen to have a large-ish stack of money at their disposal and will usually not be particularly stricken if their small-ish investment in your business doesn't pan out. They usually go for a "spray and pray" approach, investing small amounts of money for a not-insignificant percentage of equity (10% or even more). They are gambling that a small number of investments that become successful will yield them huge returns in the future.

EU-backed and state-backed investment funds are not operating under market conditions because they have a non-profit agenda to fulfil. Usually, it's to boost a certain industry in a certain country, and they don't really care what happens with the money (though their managers will swear that they do—but until they can show their results at the bottom line, don't fall for that one). They also have a "spray and pray" approach and sometimes invest in hundreds of startups each year, with little to no criteria—luckily for you.

Private wealth management funds are interesting. They are run on behalf of the very rich who do care about the returns but don't have the expertise or can't be bothered to do the investment themselves (possibly as angel investors). **Family offices** are in a similar category, but they are often more directly controlled by a single family (as the name says), and the scope of what they do for their owners is bigger.

It can be interesting to work with these types if you can find them, but this particular field is filled to the brim with fraud. There are supposed agencies that will contact you as soon as you get listed on Crunchbase, offering to introduce you to high-wealth individuals or their funds/offices in exchange for large-ish fees upfront. Personally, I recommend against signing up for services that ask for money upfront. If a "matchmaking fee" (which is realized as a percentage of the deal between the investor and you) isn't enough for them, don't even bother responding. The exception here is if you can get a good recommendation about a service from a fellow founder you trust.

CHAPTER 5   GETTING MONEY

Incubators and accelerators are related to two early phases of the startup's journey. *Incubators* should enable you to go from the idea phase to proof of concept, and *accelerators* are supposed to take you from the proof of concept phase to at least the MVP phase with paying customers, and often a bit beyond that.

What they can offer you and what they ask in return varies and can be unhelpfully creative. Some offer you "just" education and a chance to meet with some undefined investors in exchange for a small percentage of equity. Some offer you a seemingly large monetary value, sometimes hundreds of thousands of dollars, but the fine print says it's all in mentorship hours and AWS credits, while taking a significant chunk of your equity. Bonus points if that particular transaction is defined as a percentage in equity that is equal to the value of their services calculated from the pre-money valuation of your startup or some similarly creative invention[2]. Many of them are legit, though, especially those with a widely known reputation, like YC, Techstars, and 500.

VC funds are usually composed of multiple investors, either private or institutional, with different possible structures and goals. A common pattern for VC funds is that they actively invest only during a fixed number of years, usually five years, and after that, they collect a profit (if any), usually by selling their shares in companies to larger VCs.

The quality and "smartness" (in the sense of "smart money") of VCs varies so much that you should probably not hold any strong general opinions and treat each VC you encounter as a completely new species. It's common for VCs to be specialized in a certain area or industry. Try not to bother with those who are not a good match with you on that criterion.

---

[2] Think about it: if your pre-money valuation is $500,000, and they provide you with services that are valued at $100,000, you will be giving them 1/5 of your company for their services, without seeing a single cent in your bank account.

With VCs, it's often the case that you yourself need to employ the "spray and pray" approach: you're not really a startup founder if you haven't pitched to at least 100 VCs and got rejected by every single one of them.

Strategic partners are your clients who also happen to like/want what you are making so much that they will invest some money or other resources in you so you can deliver more successfully. They are very useful, and you should try to acquire some.

Pension funds and ETFs are usually where companies end up when they have existed for a long-ish time and have proven to be stable and successful. These investors don't like risk. Your company could end up with these types only after a very long time of continued existence, way past the startup phase, so don't worry about them yet.

Investors Also Have Preferences

Many investors, including VC funds, are specialized in terms of industries where they want to invest. In itself, the presence or lack of investment focus is not especially indicative of anything, but this information might help you avoid wasting time on investors who will never be interested in your startup.

It's sometime beneficial to adapt your pitch to a certain investor's sensibilities, but this requires that you invest effort into discovering how to approach them. Maybe they have a history of supporting products that have some type of social impact, and your story can be told through that lens. Maybe they favor women founders or minority founders, and it just so happens that one of the cofounders fits that description and could be the one presenting your story to the investors. Maybe they are from a part of the world that has a certain way of looking at risk and creativity, and you should woo them with your vision, or maybe they are from a very conservative part of the world and you need to attract them with numbers.

This last point is especially important for understanding the difference between high-money, high-power startup environments like San Francisco and London vs. cautious, conservative environments like Berlin and Paris. A typical stance for the first group is nicely stated in this quote from a YCombinator blog post[3]:

> *Many founders who start working on climate change solutions have no prior experience in the space. This is often a good thing for startups, as lack of experience means not paying attention to conventional wisdom—often a requirement for innovative ideas.*

There are basically no European investors who would speak or write those words. They would more likely start a call for startups with *"Required: PhD in climate sciences with 10 years+ industry experience..."*

Of course, this can complicate things for the founders. You could try min-maxing your chances and on-board cofounders who tick all such boxes, but it will soon become silly trying to find a myopic single-handed elderly woman of color to become the CFO. A healthier strategy is to start thinking in terms of "plenty of fish in the sea" and just ignore investors with whom you can't immediately achieve a fit. Alternatively, move to the part of the world that suits you more.

How to Deal with VC Funds

This is so important I will write it again: ideally, and I really mean *ideally*, if at all possible, the best way to launch any kind of a company is without external funding. This means bootstrapping it entirely with your own

---

[3] YCombinator, *"Request for Startups: Climate Tech."* www.ycombinator.com/blog/rfs-climatetech/, 12/15/2022.

funds, or at most with friends, fools, and family. You really do not want to get involved with VCs if you don't have to, and if you have to, try making it as late in the game as possible.

They will tell you otherwise, of course, and there's some merit to that. If you go with the right VC early on, they can potentially supply you with connections to other investors or clients, advice, and other non-monetary resources. These things are collectively known as *smart money*, but keep in mind the following facts of life:

- Ideally, investors like to invest in companies that don't look like they desperately need money.

- If you desperately need smart money, you will not find it.

- Everybody lies.

Unless you have extraordinarily sharp people skills, which usually come from having a lot of experience, you should trust only things that are put in ink. In other words, no matter what kind of help your investor is promising you, unless it is their obligation, written down in your contract, don't count on it, especially in the early rounds.

The reason for this is that early round investors specializing in pre-seed and seed investments are funding dozens or hundreds of startups each year with a small amount of money, just to see what works. They simply cannot spend any special effort on your startup until it gets to the "it looks like it doesn't need money" category, and you need to achieve this yourself.

Being on good terms with investors, current and potential, is good for business. You should be sending them quarterly or half-yearly reports (unless you have an explicit arrangement to do otherwise), and it's always helpful if you can wine and dine them. Keep in mind that unless you establish a personal connection with some of their team, most of them will not remember you from one quarter to the next.

CHAPTER 5   GETTING MONEY

An example report to send with copious greetings and salutations each quarter looks like this (for a B2B company):

ACME Widget Corp
Investment batch of Spring 2020
Last quarter:

- Revenue: €20,000
- Number of clients: 8

This quarter:

- Revenue: €25,000
- Number of clients: 11

EOY revenue projection: €70,000
Estimated runway: 8 months
Notable events:

- Hired a new sales employee. Now we are six total.
- We finally got the BigCorp account, our biggest client yet!
- We will be raising €1 million in Q4.

What we need from you:

- Do you know any more companies like BigCorp?

Less is more at this stage.

One question that naturally arises is, what should you do if the numbers do not look good? The optimal answer is to at least show activity on your part. Maybe you don't have revenue, but maybe you contacted 68 potential new clients and eight of them are in the process of evaluating your product. Maybe you've just joined an industry hub and will be pitching your product to the hub's members. (Note: I really mean an "industry hub" here, not a "startup hub," which are usually useless for selling your product, unless startups are your target audience—which they shouldn't be because most of them are cash starved.)

Finding Investors

Firstly, look up and talk to startup founders from your local area. They will provide you with your first leads. Next, list your startup at Crunchbase, Owler, Pitchbook, and Dealroom. Create nice LinkedIn profiles for the company and founders. Attend local startup meetups. Join foreign ones, even remote ones.

If this is your first startup, gather as much information about potential investors as you can. Later you'll be able to discern what information is important for your particular business case. Reach out to potential investors who have invested in businesses similar to yours as early as possible, but don't get particularly discouraged if they don't think you are worth investing in.

Read startup-oriented forums and threads such as from Hacker News[4] to learn from the experience of others. YCombinator (owners of the Hacker News forum) has a bunch of very useful YouTube videos[5] to learn from. Slidebean[6] is another such YouTube channel.

What to Ask Money For

Let's start this by touching on a very important special case of what *not* to ask money for: the development of a new business direction, unless you have a proven track record. Probably the worst position to be in is "what we

---

[4] https://news.ycombinator.com/item?id=33354858
[5] www.youtube.com/c/ycombinator
[6] www.youtube.com/c/Slidebean

did so far didn't work (or we didn't do anything) and we need money to try something else (i.e., to pivot)." While succeeding after pivoting is generally looked upon as good business and strong leadership, asking money for that same pivot is usually frowned upon.

A special case is asking for initial money to start working on the product, and it's with very good reason this is usually called the FFF (friends, fools, and family) phase. Unless you have a proven track record in previous businesses, you'll need a very special relationship with an investor to make them give you money at this stage.

Sometimes, incubators can help. They are organizations set up to fund and explore very early ideas (i.e., you have nothing but a PowerPoint deck) and in the EU, they are often set up by a government-related fund, so they don't even care if they're burning money. On the flip side, the amount of money they give out is minuscule, often in the range of €10,000 to €30,000, and if you're unlucky, they'll even ask you for some equity in return. Try your best to avoid this type of incubator.

The average European investor will be their happiest if they find a product that is selling like crazy in a certain area/country and the company/startup wants to expand its sales to other countries. In other words, they would like to see an already running business, with established clients, that just so happens to need more money to expand that same operation to other markets. And, of course, they would be just delighted if you didn't even take their money, just signed them up in your equity structure.

In addition to entering new markets, some good goals to ask money for (i.e., the "use of funds" box) are:

- **Increased marketing efforts with a detailed marketing plan**: Not just "We'll spend 50% on marketing" but "We'll spend 50% on customer acquisition across Google, Facebook, and native advertising to reach 40-year-old female cat lovers in Germany who show strong interest in hating dogs."

- **Increasing the value of your product/business**: Not just "We need €250k for major product improvements which will put us in a position to grow market share" but "We will spend €250k in product development to have the most sophisticated AI match-making engine in the world, raising the bar of customer satisfaction in the market."

It is understood that your projections and plans are not exact. At the very least, it's very hard to predict the future. Your goal when pitching is to be more right than wrong. If you say you need an X amount of money to do something, you should be pretty certain that you will not be wrong by more than 50% in either direction (later in business this margin of "allowed" error will shrink).

Raising money to grow your business is a chicken or the egg problem. You need money to grow your business, but everyone is looking for a startup that doesn't desperately need money so they can invest in it.

If you have a blue ocean (or blue sky) idea that isn't 100% certain to succeed, you'll find very few local investors trying to grab your attention. The European climate is way too risk-averse for that, and you'll have to go abroad, mostly to the US.

Red Flags in Investors

In theory, investors and founders have a shared goal: for the company to succeed and to make money for both. In practice, it's usually not as clear-cut as this. There are a large number of investors of all types who are oriented towards short-term goals and really don't give a damn about the companies they invest in. They usually call themselves *value investors* and are easily given to fits of fantasy, such as expecting a nascent company to immediately produce a profit.

Some additional red flags to watch for:

- Your personal network of founders, cofounders, and assorted people from the ecosystem predominantly talks trash about them. This indicates the investors do not establish quality relationships, which leaks into the business side.

- They claim to be a for-profit VC, but the majority of the money comes from a public source (like EU funds), indicating they don't care about their money and are under less pressure to make good decisions.

- They are a publicly funded investor of any type, but either a) don't ever produce a public record of the success of their investing or b) they do produce such a record but there are no significant successes in it.

- They claim that investments below €250,000 constitute a "seed" round, indicating they are unaware of the competition (again, mostly from the US) where seed rounds are often $1 million+ and €250,000 is considered an accelerator-level investment.

Unfortunately, there are many modes of failure for investors, and a successful founder is the one who has been in the business long enough that they've learned, often the hard way, what sort of people to avoid.

What to Spend Money On

If you come from a production background such as engineering, you will probably be tempted to spend almost all of the money on people who are developing the product. While there is no doubt this is the best way to create a product, it leaves aside a more important aspect of being a startup: selling it.

No one is interested in a good product that doesn't sell well. As a founder, you will have to work much harder to attract investors if you have a good product that isn't selling then if you have a less good (but still good enough) product that is already selling. Remember that engineering is about creating something fit for purpose, not perfect. And in most cases the word "fit" in a startup is related to sales.

It's not easy, but you should try to spend at least 30% of your investment on marketing and sales. If you don't know the difference between the two, hire someone who does.

What Is This Mysterious "Runway" Everyone Is Talking About?

If your startup is an airplane taking off, the runway is how many months it has before it either starts to fly or crashes because there's no more runway. This runway is made of money.

In theory, a perfect startup's journey looks like this:

1. You think of something you can sell and create (in that order).

2. You read the book called *The Mom Test* by Rob Fitzpatrick[7] (if it's not your first startup, then reread it).

3. If your idea passes the tests from the book, you quit your job and find one or two people who have the skills you don't and who are willing to work for minimum wage now in exchange for huge gains

---

[7] Rob Fitzpatrick, *The Mom Test: How to Talk to Customers & Learn if Your Business is a Good Idea When Everyone is Lying to You* (CreateSpace Independent Publishing Platform, 2013).

later. Maybe you don't know how to code or sell or do graphic design, but there are people who do, and you need to find them and bring them on board. They will be your founding team.

4. You pitch your ideas to friends, fools, and family (or incubators) and gather some initial money, let's say enough to cover the living expenses for you and your cofounders for six months.

5. All of you work your asses off during the first three months, doing three things in parallel: 1) creating the actual product, 2) onboarding future customers for the yet non-existent product, and 3) pitching your product to investors, usually angel investors and accelerators at this phase.

6. You raise early money from an angel investor or an accelerator for the following ten months and still do all of the three things mentioned above, especially the money-raising part.

7. After about six months to a year, you actually start selling the MVP of your product. Unfortunately, nothing changes at this point and all of you still do the three parallel things.

8. After a good year, you start showing enough revenue that people start referring to your business as a scaleup and you receive a seed investment that enables you to work on your product for at least 18 months (24 months if you include revenue from actual clients).

9. At this point, one of the founders finally has the time to stop working on the product and concentrate on what really matters—selling the product and raising the next round—and at that point in time the business starts to look like a success.

I'll spend a lot of time elaborating on the final point later, so just leave it as it is for now.

The steps outlined above are how your startup should work. In practice, I have never heard of or read about a startup that has worked smoothly like that.

But let's consider the runway length at various points in the above list. At step 3, your runway is literally the savings you have. Let's say that's three months. Meaning, if the next steps don't happen successfully, you're dead in the water after three months and go back to your previous life. After step 4, you have six more months. If step 6 doesn't happen, you're crashing after those six months expire. After step 6, you're good to go for another ten months, and so on. It's like playing Flappy Bird, where the game is over if you hit zero on your bank account.

In practice, founders work for free as long as they are interested in the idea and don't fall apart on a personal level. There are more examples of successful startups (please don't skip the discussion in Chapter 3 on what success means) where the founders took a large financial hit and worked for free for a long-ish period of time than those who had a perfect track record from the start and then gave up when the troubles came.

Startups have a runway that is as long as the founders are willing to stand the pressure. If there's no more money in the company's bank account, employees will be let go and/or the founders will pitch in with some more personal money, but as long as the founders are standing, the startup's doing reasonably fine. Big successes like Airbnb and Uber were in that kind of situation multiple times in their early stages.

CHAPTER 5   GETTING MONEY

This also means that if founders fold for whatever reason, the startup will naturally also fold. Ideally, all founders in the early stage should have a plan which goes something like this: "If we don't raise the next round in time and cannot pay ourselves a salary, I'll find a part-time job until we do raise it." If the founders believe in what they're trying to do, the startup will get through.

The Financial Lifecycle of a Typical VC-Backed Unicorn Startup

IBM has existed for over 100 years. It's a big, solid, boring company, and it will likely exist for another 100 years because of that (see: The Lindy effect[8]). It's the new and exciting startups that have a short life span, in some cases because they eventually get bought by the IBMs of this world. More on this later.

In the beginning, there are only founders, working their assess off for minimum or no wage at all. The company is all theirs because no one else wants it. This stage doesn't get drastically easier even if you have rich friends, fools, and family around you. It just moves the level at which you operate up or down. You still work your ass off one way or the other, because the product won't build itself, the clients won't deafen you with their loud knocking on your door, and the investors won't be sending you any love letters. In the case of the last two groups, it's probably because they don't know you exist.

After enough drinks, subtle begging, and offering different compensations in goods and services, you've managed to get a small angel investment (or an incubator investment) of €30,000 in exchange for 5% to 10% of equity. That's one of the European things. If you move to London or San Francisco, you could get five times more for two times less equity. That's just life in this part of the world. You're feeling lucky.

---

[8] Wikipedia, *"Lindy Effect,"* https://en.wikipedia.org/wiki/Lindy_effect

You join an accelerator, learn a lot, and get funded for a pre-seed round, which is slightly better than the FFF round. Let's say you receive €75,000 while the investor has bought another 10% of equity. In the accelerator, you find out that your company now has something called a *valuation* and that it's about €750,000. The founding team is now down to 85% of equity if you are lucky.

Then, a light appears—a seed round—and you think you have at least 18 months of peace and quiet to work on the product. You are wrong, of course, and the working-your-ass-off part is really just beginning, but you can dream. Oh yes, and there goes another 10% of equity, but in exchange you get €350,000 and your new post-money valuation is €3.8 million.

Your cofounders and you (jointly) are down to 75% of equity. This is still considered an early-stage startup, and your investors are likely still high-risk VCs specializing in "spraying" money and not especially caring for your company individually. You're again wondering if Europe's numerous safety nets, "free" schools, and healthcare are worth being so undervalued. At least you won't be homeless if your startup crashes because it has received too little money to compete on the global stage.

Let's say you're hailed as the next big scaleup to hit the market, your reputation precedes you, you're bigger than the Beatles, and you go to the first "serious" funding round called a "series A", with a valuation of €50 million, and the company receives €15 million in cash for another 30% of equity. Your founders' equity falls to 45% and now things change.

Big decisions are now usually made by the board of directors where investors jointly have the majority. Few startups managed to avoid this, most notably Facebook, where Mark Z. managed to negotiate a veto power over everyone. If it's good for Mark Z., it's good for you too.

At this stage, your investor is a moderately large VC fund or a group of VC funds that only invest in established businesses meeting certain bottom-line criteria. You are establishing offices internationally. Your investors at this point are probably non-European.

CHAPTER 5 GETTING MONEY

Since the founders as a group are now a minority shareholder, the board decides to move for a series B, where everyone's share goes down by another 20% proportionally in favor of a new VC, which brings in €50 million in cash, and your valuation is a quarter of the way to becoming a unicorn.

Another decision in the ripeness of time gets you to a series C, a €220 million investment for another 20% of the equity in the same way, and as your valuation because of that is €1.1 billion, you now have a genuine unicorn on your hands—and 5% to 10% of the original equity you personally started with as a founder. Congratulations! If you exit now and sell everything, you'll leave with €55 million to €110 million in your pocket (minus taxes).

As the investment rounds progress, the investors get progressively less fond of risk but bring in more money. In later rounds, shares in the company get bought by hedge funds, investment banks, private equity firms, and even some pension funds.

The longer the company exists and is successful, the more of its shares are bought by financial behemoths, which pick their investments based on how boring they are (which is a good thing in their context). For example, the top six IBM owners are The Vanguard Group, State Street Global Advisors, BlackRock Fund Advisors, Vanguard Total Stock Market Index, Vanguard 500 Index Fund, and the SPDR S&P 500 ETF Trust.

For now, you are a long way away from those kinds of worries. What you should do is have a table like this pinned on a wall somewhere in your office as a roadmap:

Time	Valuation	Round equity	Round cash	Founders %[9]
Year 1 – FFF	€300,000	5%	€15,000	95%
Year 2 – Accelerator	€750,000	10%	€75,000	85%
Year 3 – Seed	€3,500,000	10%	€350,000	75%
Year 4 – A	€50,000,000	30%	€15,000,000	45%
Year 5 – B	€220,000,000	20%	€50,000,000	36%
Year 6 – C	€1,100,000,000	20%	€220,000,000	28%

Every startup has a different path, and your valuations and rounds will vary, but the point is that you absolutely must keep an eye on your valuation because it dictates what kinds of investors your startup will attract and what the final outcome might be.

Here's an example: in the above table, if three founders decide to sell out and exit after series A (and the market and the investors are in favor of their decision, of course, which they won't be because the company still depends on the founders at this stage), they will exit with 45% equity, which is theoretically worth €22.5 million. Split evenly three ways, that's €7.5 million each. If they decide to exit after series B, that's over €26 million each. After series C, that's €102 million each.

Note that skipping rounds can be seen as a sign of slow growth or unambitious founders. If you are committed to the VC game, you pretty much need to keep raising on schedule, or be so successful it doesn't matter.

Founders exiting from the startup is often a sign that things are not going too well, because the founders are the maniacs who created the company from thin air and their own blood, sweat, and tears—and no one else can work that hard. Even in acquisitions, there are usually contractual

---

[9] Founders are here considered as a group. If there are three founders in the group and they split evenly, each of them has a little over 9% of equity after series C.

rules that the original startup founders remain in the company as "heads of division" for a good number of years to ensure the newly acquired division stays on track.

Rules of the Game

One source of possible problems can be various conditions and rules some VCs try to impose on the startup. The rule of thumb here is that you don't have to agree to anything you don't want to. There are no "usual" or "standard" rules you have to accept.

Typically, early stage VCs will request veto power over hiring C-level employees or purchases over a certain amount or even bank loans and will request setting a salary cap for founders and such. While these kinds of controls might even be useful in the very early stages of an inexperienced startup (or at least neutral, since you don't have enough money to do serious damage anyway), they are usually a nuisance at seed and later stages.

What's more potentially problematic at later stages are claims to special treatment in some financial matters. In the US, companies can issue *preferred stock*, which is understood to mean shares in companies that are first on the list when profits are distributed, or debt is settled, but in return carry no voting power. By crafting special rules for themselves, VCs can reduce the amount of money that ends up in the founders' pockets on exit.

One example of a dangerous rule is that if a company is sold for a less than expected price, and the VCs would receive a proportional portion of the sale price which is lesser than the total sum of their investments, investment contracts might be set up in a way that the VCs get at least the full sum they invested, and this money is taken out of the founders' portion of the exit sum. There are examples of startups where the VCs got the majority vote, sold the company for less than the founders wanted to sell because they needed the money quickly, and then siphoned almost all of the founders' proportional shares of the sales to cover their losses.

Some examples of sketchy investment contract rules are:

- VCs might require that any dividend distribution event first covers their investment amount before the rest is distributed among the shareholders.

- VCs might require that any liquidation event (in which the whole company is sold) first covers a multiple of their investment (e.g., they could be guaranteed to a two or three times the return on their investment when the company gets sold, regardless of how much stock they hold).

- VCs could try to impose "penalties" in additional equity or cash if important milestones are not reached before the next round is raised.

- VCs might introduce "liquidity preference" in your contract which determines the order and the amount they get paid in the event of an exit, in order to secure some level of protection of their assets in the event a startup fails or exits with a loss. This might also include non-money assets such as equipment.

Rules like these are usually crafted to reduce the risk to the investors but remember the rule of thumb: you do not have to agree to any of them. Negotiation is crucial.

Other common requirements are

- **Drag-along**: In case of a buyout, the majority shareholder can force the minority shareholder to sell their part under the same conditions (makes the sale easier if the buyer wants to buy 100% of the company).

- **Tag-along**: In case of a buyout, the minority shareholder can force the sale of their own shares together with the majority shareholder's shares under the same conditions (allows the minority shareholder to exit under the same condition as the majority shareholder).

- **Non-dilution**: Disallows transactions where a new investor buys a fixed percentage of the total company (e.g., if the company creates new shares out of thin air), diluting all existing owners' share percentage by a certain ratio (pro-rata). Small investors often put this clause in the investment agreement, but most of them are aware that future big investors will squeeze them out if a big investment happens.

- **Pre-emptive rights**: If a shareholder intends to sell their shares, they must offer them to other currently existing shareholders first, under the same conditions that a third party is offering for them.

A special consideration must always be made for the difference between the company and the founders (as discussed in the section on the corporate veil).

Since the company is its own legal entity, a law firm hired to protect the interests of the company might not (and actually shouldn't) protect the interests of the founders. This is true even in European countries which otherwise aren't yet fully onboard with capitalism.

When Diligence Is Due

One crucial step taken before investors commit is the *due diligence (DD) process* in which they check if the company is in the condition promised. If you claim the company has no debt, they check that. If you claim you employ a number of people, they check that. If you claim a certain revenue, they check that. Be nice during this process. It's usually fair.

One part of the DD process is to enumerate all of the company's assets and liabilities, and this includes all obligations to third parties such as FFF investors and ex-founders.

If you as founders made a deal to return some of the FFF investment money to the respective investors, this should be clearly visible in the results of DD. The same is true if you need to finish paying out some of the early cofounders or partners.

The Eastern European Perspective on Company Shares

In more business-friendly parts of the world, when the company gets incorporated, some company shares are created and assigned to the founders. Let's say there are 1,000 initial shares equally split between two founders, so each gets 500 shares and has 50% equity in the company. When the company receives an investment, new shares are created out of thin air by the company, and the investor gets those shares in exchange for money being transferred to the company. Each of the founders still has the same number of shares as before, but they are worth less than before. This is called *dilution*.

In this company, say a new investor comes and buys 10% of equity. The company creates 111 brand new shares and issues them to the investor. The original founders have exactly the same number of shares as before, but the percentage of equity those shares represent is reduced to 45% each.

CHAPTER 5 GETTING MONEY

This works fine in parts of the world where creating the type of company that can issue shares like that is normal. Because of historical reasons, this usually is not the case in Eastern Europe. Here, you are lucky if you live in a country that has reasonably modern (as in, it has been updated in the last 50 years) laws governing limited liability companies (LLCs).

These kinds of companies do not have "shares" in the same way US corporations do, and this is important since most educational materials out there assume the US way of doing things. The Eastern European variants often have bizarre rules regarding accounting, ownership rights, transfers, and the number and structure of shares.

For example, the Croatian variant of the LLC (which is the DOO) can have shares of uneven, arbitrary value, but the value of individual shares cannot be lower than €10, and on top of that, the fees for many bureaucratic operations rise with the number of shares. Investments that result in equity shifts could be done in a way that leaves the company with a strange structure of shares on paper that does not accurately represent the agreed-upon ownership percentage, with additional wording in the shareholders agreement that the parties will behave "as if" the ownership shares are such-and-such.

With weird laws like this, good lawyers are a must-have. You basically have no chance of decoding what can and cannot be done within legal limits, not to mention how. What's even weirder is that corporate lawyers can't help you because they are dealing with a completely different form of a company (DD), so you really need to find someone who has experience with startups.

Assuming that you do have a lawyer that can be trusted to work around possible issues, the end result will be a more or less accurate simulation of what the US system does by default: new shares will be created somehow, and the right parties will end up with the right shares. The investors will be able to transfer money to the company in some more-or-less weird way (depending on the country), and your shares will be diluted.

Note that there are significant differences in how employees can receive company stock (ESOP), which is discussed in Chapter 7.

How Can Founders Make Money?

The question naturally arises: how can founders make money in an equity-for-investment transaction?

In more business-friendly parts of the world, it is common that founders also offer some of their shares to sell to the investors, instead of having the company create all of the investors' shares out of thin air (which is the "normal way"). In the early stages and in the case where shares are exactly equal in value and rights, a typical investment transaction involves having the company create a number of new shares, to which the investors pitch in with a number of their own personal shares, and the investor gets to own just a pile of shares. They don't care where the shares come from.

Because of the legislative weirdness, this might not be as easy in Eastern Europe. Find a good lawyer.

One more thing is worth noting: the mind games played between the investors and the founders often involve looking down on founders selling their own personal shares. The official reason is that founders who sell their personal shares have less "skin in the game" in the company and don't work as hard to make the company succeed, as they can instead take the money and enjoy life a bit more than before. You should consider for yourself if it's worth doing business with investors who hold that kind of opinion. (See also the discussion on founders' salaries later in this book.)

CHAPTER 5   GETTING MONEY

> **PERSONAL EXAMPLE #1: LOSING OUT ON EU FUNDING BECAUSE WE DIDN'T GET AN INTERNATIONAL TRADEMARK**

At one time we applied to an EU funding call. It involved having to prove that there was at least one employee working full-time for the company, and that we had a certain amount of cash, since the proposal was for projects of a certain minimal value in euros and the EU funded 60%-80% of that.

We lost that funding by a single point because even though we knew one of the criteria was IP protection and we trademarked our name specifically for this reason, it turned out we had to protect it *internationally*, not in our local country, even though it was not documented as such in the call document. It was literally the only item in the checklist where we were assessed with 0 points. International protection is, naturally, more expensive than just the local one.

> **PERSONAL EXAMPLE #2: ALMOST GETTING TRICKED BY AN ONLINE ACCELERATOR INTO GIVING NEARLY 20% OF EQUITY**

The footnote about an accelerator giving $100.000 in services and various cloud credits in exchange for a huge chunk of our equity is not made up! It all started with a cold e-mail where a legit-looking online accelerator introduced themselves and made an interesting offer in terms of education and investment opportunities. I was close to signing the contract with them and my cofounders also approved of the idea, but then I decided to reread it just one more time before I signed it. And what I found out was a piece of text buried in an un-obvious place that would trigger in case of an investment and would have bound us to transfer the portion of our equity to the accelerator equal to the value of the services they provided, calculated from the *pre-money valuation*.

At that time, the company was valuated at around €640.000, and the accelerator calculated the value of their services to $100.000, which means we would have lost more than 15% of equity to them.

I brought the issue up on our next call and they essentially said "yeah, but we don't enforce it." They refused my proposal to take this text out of the contract since they don't enforce it, and that was my last communication with them.

This particular event is baffling because the chance of them winning out with the strategy of strangling the startups they invest in is basically zero. It just doesn't make good business sense from either side.

CHAPTER 6

Guest Chapter: On Startup Valuations (and Other Dark Stories)

By Božidar Pavlović

TL;DR

- Early stage startup company valuations are subjective. Your job as a founder is to negotiate the biggest valuation you can.
- Term sheets specify the terms under which the investment could happen, but they do not constitute an investment agreement.
- Always be raising.
- You need to be skillful, smart, and ready to fail (and then get up and try again).

CHAPTER 6   GUEST CHAPTER: ON STARTUP VALUATIONS (AND OTHER DARK STORIES)

So, you have a company, and you fondly call it a startup. There are already some paying users. In other words, certain people do like your product or service and are willing to pay for using it . . . but the initial money (seed capital) is nearly gone. You are soon to spend the last nickel and dime you borrowed from your parents and friends. Do you need to keep paying the salaries? Hire more skilled people? Pay the sales commission? Invest in marketing? Facebook or Google ads, anyone?

If this is the case, the moment for you to start thinking about external financing is long overdue, my friend.

There are several ways to attract capital so your company can grow. One of the most common ways is by giving away part of your company's ownership (equity) in return for, well, money. It's not easy, though. It is in your best interest to give away as little equity as possible for the maximum amount of money, while the investor wants as much ownership as possible for the given amount of money. That's where the valuation process kicks in.

But before diving deeper into valuation musings, let's briefly discuss some best practices for fundraising.

The 5W Rule

As in every good whodunit mystery and crime thriller, the best way to start is with the 5W rule: *Why? Who? Where? What? When?*

Since we have already (kind of) answered the Why (that is, why we need the money), let's talk about the Who first.

Who?

Fundraising itself doesn't necessarily mean taking money exclusively from the vulture/venture capitalists who could rip you off. Sometimes your grandparents have some extra money under their mattress and are

CHAPTER 6   GUEST CHAPTER: ON STARTUP VALUATIONS (AND OTHER DARK STORIES)

willing to help you. There are friends and other family members who have believed in your integrity ever since you were selling seashells on the seashore.

Crowdfunding very often works quite well, especially when your product appeals to the wider public (and if you promise some perks). Maybe there are interesting credit lines for founders and startups funded by the EU or the local banks. Joining the incubator (which might give you utilities for free or with reduced pricing) also works.

So explore your options before you start looking for VC money, but please do not put your house under mortgage to fund your startup. Ever.

Where?

When it comes to fundraising, first you have to look around at the local ecosystem. Domestic and regional VCs are obvious choices. They know the operating space, they know other founders, they know what's going on around here, and they can utilize their network connections, open some doors for you, and help you out with advice.

Going abroad is a good move only after you have exhausted all your local options. However, you have to realize that the big investment funds from abroad have adequately huge target lists, and you will be competing with lots of other super sexy startups from all around the world. And I really mean lots of them.

What?

What could you get instead of VC money? You could get a convertible loan (for which you pay regular interest) and this loan can be exchanged for equity in the next investment round.

You can also hire people to work for minimal salary, but in exchange you can give them shares or options in your company (at the moment this not too easy in Croatia, but this will hopefully change for the better).

CHAPTER 6 GUEST CHAPTER: ON STARTUP VALUATIONS (AND OTHER DARK STORIES)

But once you make up your mind to get the VC money, you better start looking around, establishing connections, and presenting your company because you will surely not sign the first deal that comes knocking at your door. This is a long and painful process, but you must be aware that, ultimately, you're looking for a cofounder. You should treat the chosen VC like one, and the VC should treat you equally.

When?

This is easy: when you are fully ready! Do your own research. Don't rush, and make sure to investigate all the potential roads before actually going out to VCs.

Once you go there, it's like the Ten Commandments. Be 100% ready to defend your business model with proper and solid arguments, know thy numbers by heart, explain your product-market fit in detail, know thy competition, practice your pitch regularly, and keep refining your deck on a daily basis. Understand the language of the small print and terms and conditions and talk to mentors and friends. There are many capable people out there willing to help you with free advice.

Valuation

The dry definition goes like this: "Valuation is a quantitative process of determining the fair value of an asset or a firm."[1]

In reality, especially with startups and companies with not too many physical assets, it is hard to determine a fair value. (Asset-light companies have no servers, buildings, or other physical goods in their balance sheet; they have mostly their own software. In other words, they own just the intellectual property.)

---
[1] www.investopedia.com/terms/v/valuation.asp

CHAPTER 6   GUEST CHAPTER: ON STARTUP VALUATIONS (AND OTHER DARK STORIES)

You could use the direct valuation method (the company has limited KPI reports that might not reflect the company's true potential) or try the relative valuation method (comparison with similar companies) but usually it's a combination of both. That's why the valuation process usually takes a lot of time and involves a ping-pong of arguments between potential investors and founders.

Ultimately, the valuation should be a concrete number everybody's satisfied with. Founders will not become too diluted, and the investors will become partial owners of the business whose potential they believe in.

Only after the valuation and the investment amount is mutually agreed upon (which leads us to the percentage of ownership to be transferred to investors, i.e., the term sheet is agreed and signed), only then should the proper funding paperwork begin, the lawyers' brigade be summoned, and the nerves be hardened.

The basic, nonbinding document that covers the agreement is called the term sheet. We'll discuss the term sheet later, but before that, it's important to understand that the external funding process is often repetitive, which means you'll go through it again in a few years. That's why it's essential to take care of and keep thinking of the valuation itself. It grows (as does the company's real value) with the growth of the overall business and should be frequently revisited, but surely before the next funding round.

Very often people get confused about the terms "pre-money" and "post-money" valuation, but the explanation is pretty straightforward. Before you get the agreed amount of money (let's call it Y), the agreed (pre-money) valuation is set to X. After you receive the money, the new, post-money valuation is X + Y. The pre-money valuation, however, should reflect the fair value of the company, as discussed earlier, and is used to calculate the share of equity (ownership) the founders are giving up for the capital injection.

For example, the pre-money valuation is set to €10 million, and the founders are looking for a €2 million investment. They will be giving up (selling) 20% of the company equity (shares) in return for €2 million cash. After the actual transaction takes place, the company's post-money valuation is €12 million.

The Term Sheet

So, let's get things straight, since it's ambiguous. A term sheet is indeed a contract but ultimately it's non-binding. That means you (or the investor, or both) can chicken out without going any further. In other words, the term sheet only outlines the terms (*term* sheet, get it?) and conditions of a potential investment deal.

But the devil is in the details. OK, you agreed on the company's perceived value, but what happens with the risk? What if your company goes south, not because of your immaculate idea, but because of, say, faster competition, supply chain problems, recession, inflation, stagnation, stagflation, earthquake, pandemics, World War Three, Armageddon, zombie apocalypse? As we've learned in recent years, anything is possible.

Well, my friends, this is the reason why investors want to introduce as many safety mechanisms as possible to your term sheet, providing for any possible scenario. Very often this is written in complex legalese, small print, wrapped around hard-to-understand phrases, so the best advice is (again) to do your own research, ask for external advice, and try to understand the specifics of your term sheet.

On the other hand, there is a thing called the liquidity event that everybody's secretly praying for. This is the end of the road for you as a founder. It's either an IPO (initial public offering, a fancy name for the listing on a stock exchange), a merger with some other company, or an acquisition of your company by a bigger fish. In other words, the liquidity event enables the founders and investors to cash out.

CHAPTER 6   GUEST CHAPTER: ON STARTUP VALUATIONS (AND OTHER DARK STORIES)

Sometimes the bag of money is not deep enough, so it's also important to define who gets the money first (also known as liquidation preference), which is defined in the term sheet. There are also all sorts of measures or safety mechanisms (mentioned earlier) that cover each side's rights and obligations in case of (God forbid!) default, valuation decrease, or any significant business event that might lead to money loss.

With every subsequent (future) investment, the founders and the previous investors get diluted, but not necessarily. There are ways to limit the dilution, or at least keep the same or similar level of rights, especially in case of down-round (i.e., if the future valuation will be lower than today's, as is currently the case in the market). That's why term sheets usually include certain anti-dilutive provisions.

Quite often, the equity you sell brings an additional benefit to the investors: the right to vote. This is usually addressed in the term sheet, but you have to be aware that it's a powerful weapon. The voting rights might influence important decisions in the company.

The lesson here is that a good term sheet document should at least include the agreed company valuation, investment amount, percentage stake, voting rights, liquidation preference, anti-dilutive provisions, and investor's commitment.

Conclusion

The moral of this story: looking for an external investment is a long and tiring journey, full of obstacles, but the outcome can be extremely powerful and satisfying. If you manage to find the right partners with the right mindset (and the right contacts) it can enable your company to rise to unthinkable heights. But you need to be skillful, smart, and ready to fail.

CHAPTER 6   GUEST CHAPTER: ON STARTUP VALUATIONS (AND OTHER DARK STORIES)

> **PERSONAL EXAMPLE: EVERY STARTUP NEEDS A CFO**
>
> As a mentor, my main gripe about startup finances is that without a CFO (i.e., someone whose sole responsibility is to track what's going on with money), startups often spend too much and founders have little to no exact insight on where the money goes. Startups should really hire a CFO as soon as possible, even if it's a part-time or occasional role. It's not only about spending too much; it's also about not understanding when the money will be available on their accounts and not understanding the dynamics of their tax obligations. I've seen startups get in a lot of trouble because they didn't have a CFO, so get one ASAP.

CHAPTER 7

Your Company is the Average of Its Founders

TL;DR

- If you can't get optimal people early on, at least be aware of their (and your) weak points.
- Corporate culture is formed from the founders' habits.
- Hard work increases the likelihood of luck finding you. Hard work also prepares you for when it does.
- Being transparent about the company operations and finances helps a great deal in the early stages.
- Remote working is a blessing and a curse. Don't fall for propaganda on either side.

CHAPTER 7   YOUR COMPANY IS THE AVERAGE OF ITS FOUNDERS

If You Need to Make Mistakes in Choosing Cofounders, Be Aware of Them in Advance

Most of us must balance the desire to work on something cool with the need to pay daily bills. Until we reach financial independence, there will always be compromises. Unfortunately, the startup climate is really harsh with the demands on founders' time. Basically, founders need to be so dedicated to the company that they will consciously and willingly disregard everything else, at least temporarily. This is why it's hard to find good cofounders and why it's difficult to onboard one if they have not been there to share the initial enthusiasm.

The rates of divorce, depression, and addictive disorders among successful startup founders are atrocious. It's an unfortunate but true stereotype that founders neglect their families and their health for their company to succeed. We could lament over that fact, but it's still a fact. Even founders with a good start plus rich parents and friends often burn out in the early days, so what they do as a startup is not just about the money. It cannot be about the money. It must be about the passion.

Reconsider if you have cofounders who won't work for free.

All startups should have an agreement that cofounders will actively work on the startup for N years before realizing their claim on the equity. If they bail out early, you can reallocate the equity. Having founders holding equity but providing no services to the company is harmful to the company.

Even if you are on good terms with your cofounders, you need to have that type of a contract, because circumstances often change unexpectedly. People's priorities can change drastically with marriage, newborn children, sickness in the family, or just bad luck.

If you have doubts that the cofounder you are wooing will stick with you until the end, your duty as a "first" founder is to make a contract with them so it doesn't harm the company if they leave. You should have contingency plans to replace them.

CHAPTER 7 YOUR COMPANY IS THE AVERAGE OF ITS FOUNDERS

Do not pick a founder with whom you cannot comfortably work in person. Online-only cofounders do not work. Contrasted to Americans, Europeans on average are not as accustomed to travelling around and there are significant cultural differences, especially around business, everywhere you go. Communication often fails if a part of the founding team lives on the other side of the country, let alone in another country.

A founder who is great in an early role might not be good in a later one. CTOs especially. A CTO who can hack together a working MVP for a complex SaaS product by themselves in a couple of months is exactly the wrong person to have when you get to the phase where you need to hire a team of people to continue working on the product. If they can't handle being a leader, create a nice cushy R&D department outside the company's normal operations for them so they can continue doing what they love and occasionally create something wonderful that simply wouldn't get created in a more structured team.

If you are not a frequent visitor at a major tech hub, it's likely you will not be able to find a good cofounder when you first start looking. That could be ok, as long as you find someone good enough for the first leg of the journey.

Of course, you should be realistic about what you and that person can do and under what conditions can you operate smoothly. Make a written contract that explicitly states what happens when/if one of you doesn't want to continue.

It is not unusual to find successful startups that have gone through one or two iterations of cofounders. In fact, I know a successful startup (really a scaleup at this point) that went through close to a dozen cofounders until the right team was in place. One main founder was really persistent and ultimately lucky to recognize and get the people he needed to continue.

A red flag for a company, as far as most VCs are concerned, is if there are founders in the cap table of the company who are absent from its daily runnings. Be nice and fair to those who leave. Agree on monetary compensation if you can.

CHAPTER 7   YOUR COMPANY IS THE AVERAGE OF ITS FOUNDERS

Corporate Culture Is Made of Founders' Habits

By the very nature of what they need to do (i.e., everything), founders are often *not* team workers. They must do a mountain of highly demanding work, and if they don't do it, no one will. Here's why: cofounders are usually picked to complement each other in skills. If a tech-oriented cofounder stops being productive, the marketing-savvy one cannot fill their shoes (and vice versa). Founders work together, but often not on the same aspects of the business and often can't make accommodations for each other's minor problems. They need to work together efficiently, and each one needs to have a no-bullshit approach with the other.

However, if you propagate this culture when it's time to hire people, you will have a bad time! You want a team that will work on achieving your vision, not a bunch of cowboy individuals who, while excellent in their areas of expertise, think they can run the company for you—in a different way than you. Herding cats, while possible, is not productive.

The usual way this gets resolved is that the founding team becomes management and they internally maintain a special relationship not really possible or even tolerated in newcomers (however, treat the newcomers fairly or they will leave). Whether you can avoid this and make it happen another way is up to you.

Read management books like *Work the System* by Sam Carpenter[1] to get a clue on how to organize people. Learn to delegate. As your company grows from one stage to the next, you will need to find or groom people

---

[1] Sam Carpenter, *Work the System: The Simple Mechanics of Making More and Working Less (4th Edition)* (Austin, TX: Greenleaf Book Group Press, 2021).

to do what you did in the previous stage so you can be free to do things required for the success of the company in the next stage—things you don't even know will be required of you.

Unfortunately, the skills that make one a good entrepreneur do not necessarily make that someone a good manager. The former is about cherry-picking good ideas, recognizing market opportunities, charming investors, and negotiating deals; the latter is about making people happy while they do the things you want them to do. As soon as you have the money, hire professional managers.

The personal skills most valuable in founders are

- **Consistent and active communication**: It can skew business deals in your direction. It can even "fix" problems with the product.

- **Sales (related to the above)**: The founders are selling each other the vision, the investors the business opportunity, the employees the lifestyle, and the customers the solution to their problems.

- **Perseverance, or tenacity:** The startup will basically remain active/alive as long as the founders are willing to endure.

Note that technical expertise isn't on the list. Not that it isn't important, but it's only a top priority if the company is actually a research lab and will never ever interact with end users in any way (and it's hard to be a lab as a startup because the set of potential customers is usually tiny). At most, a single founder (usually the CTO) should be technically brilliant.

CHAPTER 7   YOUR COMPANY IS THE AVERAGE OF ITS FOUNDERS

Remote Work Is Like a Potent Spice. Use It Sparingly.

While some people swear remote working (i.e., working from home) makes them more productive than visiting an office daily, many companies have found it brings them an overall reduction in team cohesion and productivity. Homes usually have too many distractions and can get very boring if you spend a lot of time in them.

Ultimately, it's up to the individual companies and their employees to decide. From what I've seen, companies that do remote work the best have some kind of a hybrid arrangement, like "you can work ten working days a month from home, and you pick which ones, but you have to announce them at least two days in advance, and if there's a meeting, you must attend it from any location you happen to be in."

This is not to say there aren't successful examples of companies doing all-remote work, of course. Again, it's up to the specific company to decide.

In the very early stages, it's tempting, and sometimes unavoidable because of financial reasons, to hire remote freelancers on a per-project basis. This can most efficiently be done through global platforms such as Toptal, Upwork, Revelo, and others.

If you are in need of groups of developers, you should check if there are development agencies in your environment where you can hire entire teams, including project designers and managers. In the Adriatic region, some of the agencies that operate in this way are Degordian, Bornfight, and Q Agency. Their prices will usually not be significantly lower than those on the global platforms because everyone in the western-facing world is competing for the same talent and the same clients, but this approach has one significant advantage: you can work much more closely with such a team because of the ability to meet some of them in person (this is a significant advantage in most cases!) and because of the same cultural inclinations.

On Transparency

In the early days, when it's just you and your cofounders, or a couple of early employees, it's far less stressful for everyone if you can be as transparent as possible with everyone involved about business deals, financial deals, and everything else that is going on with the company. It is often the decent thing to do as well, since they can decide for themselves if they want to stick around and why, and it builds trust.

You can afford to be secretive (like many corporations are, often for valid reasons) when you get to be big, but not in the early stages (which, again, might take years).

Some rules of thumb to follow here are

- Avoid generating too many expectations of your team, which can lead to frustration if things don't materialize and will impact team morale. But do encourage them and be as enthusiastic as possible.

- Always provide context so the team can better understand how and why events took place and decisions were made.

- Think preemptively. Put yourself into your team's shoes and try to address doubts that may arise from your communication upfront.

- Always give space for clearing doubts and follow up with your staff to assess the impact of your communication. You'd be surprised at how many ways people can react to the same information.

The flip side of sharing too much can be that people you share the information with will undoubtedly give you their opinion and that might lead you to second-guess yourself. As a founder, you will have to make dozens of decisions every day, and you don't want to be dragged down or delayed because of indecision. And for the team, they should be focused on building the product in accordance with your vision—not worrying about the bank account.

Again, it's up to individual founders and employees to reach a satisfactory status quo and ensure smooth operation.

The Option Pool and Vesting

When the company is created, the founders own every share of it. Investors then buy their way into the cap table with their investments. But there are others who could and probably should get a piece of the company: the employees.

Companies usually set aside a certain percentage of the company equity to be distributed to early employees, and that's called the option pool. If the company is set up as an LLC, it can't own its own shares, so the option pool is generally set up via an agreement between cofounders and its shares are temporarily owned by one or more employees.

Especially in the early days, equity can serve as motivation if you cannot pay the expected wages to your employees—and as an early startup, you probably can't. The amount of equity varies wildly, from 0.1% to 5%, depending on the circumstances. In the more developed economies, many highly skilled workers and freelancers help startups by charging less than their usual rates, compensating the rest with a small percentage of equity. It's not rare to encounter UX designers and developers who have accumulated tiny percentages from dozens of startups in the hope that some of them will pay out big in the future.

When employees are expected to work more or less full-time for the company while receiving a regular salary, you, as a founder, will want to protect the company from early abandonment by crucial employees. This is similar to the discussion about cofounders: inactive equity holders are detrimental to the company, as every bit of equity you sell leaves you with less and less maneuvering space.

The process of giving away equity as a bonus to employees, prolonged over a certain time to ensure employees don't leave, is commonly called *vesting*. The contract where the employees receive equity can (and should!) be worded in a way that releases the equity to them in multi-year stages. For example, if the employee is promised 1% of the total equity, they might receive this in batches of 0.2% every six months, or whatever the business circumstances might allow.

Another term for this, especially in big established corporations, is the Employee Stock Ownership Plan (ESOP). It is often described as an employee benefits plan, which is a win-win for everyone: employees know that they will enjoy a share in the company's success and are motivated to contribute to this success, and the owners (founders) are interested in having motivated employees.

However you call it, note that employees with equity are not your cofounders (unless you really want to label them as such).

Waiting for ESOP in Europe

As described previously, ESOP stands for Employee Stock Ownership Plan and it is a set of policies that ultimately enable employees to own a share of the business they work for.

The US has a long tradition of giving employees shares in the company and several common frameworks for doing so. It even has a different concept with the same acronym (Employee Stock Options Plan). Then there's ESPP (Employee Share Purchase Plan), which is something very different. Most startups just call it *option vesting* and are done with it. Alas, it is not that simple in Europe.

CHAPTER 7   YOUR COMPANY IS THE AVERAGE OF ITS FOUNDERS

Even though European countries are mostly strong on social programs of wealth redistribution, they are curiously tight on both creating entrepreneurs and enabling employees to, in some way, own portions of their companies. Here are some key differences between the regions:

- There are about 15 million employee owners in the US, but about 10x less in Europe[2].

- Europe is apparently really pushing for the ESOP idea, which is suitable for big companies that can afford the bureaucracy, while it's much more common for US startups to use the conceptually simpler method of options vesting. The difference is that the ESOP idea includes actual, permanent ownership of stock, while options are usually just a means to immediately sell an amount of stock on behalf of the employee once the company goes public.

- **Tax timing:** In the US, for incentive stock options (the ones used by startups), the biggest tax event is when the exercised stocks are sold. No taxes are due when the stocks are granted. In most European countries, the worst of which are Belgium and Germany[3], stock options are taxed at the point of grant. This basically means employees are not only "rewarded" with uncertain stock options, but they must also pay taxes for this privilege.

---

[2] Academia, David Ellerman, "A Generic ESOP: Employee Share Plan for Europe," www.academia.edu/44213460/A_Generic_ESOP_Employee_Share_Plan_for_Europe

[3] Index Ventures, "*Rewarding Talent: A guide to stock options for European entrepreneurs,*" www.indexventures.com/rewardingtalent/handbook.

Transferring shares of ownership works fine in basically any jurisdiction, but there are usually problems of varying severity with taxes. The "good" countries (the top three are Latvia, Lithuania, and Estonia) tax options at the point of sale, with the condition that they are held for a certain amount of time before selling. The sale is taxed as capital gains.

For example, the Estonian Tax and Customs Board expects an option agreement to be tied to the actual employment agreement that has to last at least three years for the options to be exempt from being regarded as salary and not taxed with anything other than income tax (otherwise social security taxes and such will be demanded from the company).

Since this is highly country-specific, it is an area where you should seek expert advice from both accountants and lawyers (since usually they only know their half of the story).

Cases where ESOPs are actually implemented as intended by startups in Europe are still rare, as are cases where startups are established as corporations with actual shares instead of as LLCs. Hopefully, this will change.

PERSONAL EXAMPLE: IN SEARCH FOR THE PERFECT TEAM

Equinox Vision is currently on its third iteration of cofounders, with me being the only persistent member over the years. It's just how things happened. First, I assembled an unofficial "PoC team," which included friends and acquaintances, before the company was even established. We managed to produce something resembling the core of the idea and worked on the initial branding. After slightly more than a year of that, and just as this team started to seriously lose its momentum, the first "true" VC fund opened in Croatia and, after amicably parting ways with all members of this team except the CTO and CMO, the three of us started a company and got a tiny investment to get things going. The development was slow and the funds ran out quickly, so first the CTO had to leave for medical reasons and then the CMO left, but during this phase we managed to produce an MVP and had our first real, recurring customers. Now my cofounder is a colleague who shares the CMO and COO roles, and I'm sharing the CEO and CTO roles. We just finished producing a product that resembles my original vision from four years ago, and our revenue graph is actually becoming hockey-stick-ish.

My main point is that sometimes it's necessary to part ways with cofounders to be able to move forward, and you shouldn't be afraid of this. Be kind and fair and pay out your ex-cofounder as needed. My second point is that unless you're sitting on a mountain of cash, prepare for slow progress, but also for a hockey-stick growth.

CHAPTER 8

Guest Chapter: Recruiting in a Startup Environment

By Mario Mucalo

TL;DR

- Think hard about which kind of skills you need from your early employees.
- Be present in social circles, social networks, and media, especially those frequented by your potential employees.
- Be honest in what you want from your employees.
- Do not trust third parties to select your early employees, ever.
- Always be ready to quickly fire people who are not contributing to your vision.

CHAPTER 8 GUEST CHAPTER: RECRUITING IN A STARTUP ENVIRONMENT

I've been a member of a startup for the last four years. Before that, I was working in a US startup for five years. We have been very lucky with recruiting people . . . at times. We have also had situations where we were not so lucky. So, I'd love to share my two cents on how I approach recruiting in a startup.

First of all, it depends on whether you're already well-funded and can afford competitive salaries and other perks that go with it, or not. Since we've never really been in such a situation, I cannot talk about that side of the story, although most points outlined here should apply.

I am talking about recruiting in environments where you cannot afford the best possible conditions on the market for a new hire and need to find other ways of attracting amazing people.

Recruiting Starts Well Before the Recruiting Actually Starts

You are looking for a person to fill a position and do an amazing job in that role. You either ask around your network or you put out an opening and see who applies.

But then you hit a brick wall. Nobody looks at your position. No good people are applying. When you say to people, "Would you like to work with us?" they are reluctant, because no one has ever heard of you!

If you're in a startup, you need to make people aware of what you do. Doing this today is easier than ever, as there are so many sites and media companies out there that are dedicated to startups, and startups are sexy to write about, even for the mainstream media. Also, you can always leverage the power of social networks in your favor.

But in order to do that, you need to do it consistently, not only when you need to have people hear of you. For example, our founder gave himself the challenge to write on LinkedIn every day and has done that for three years[1]. Some posts were his own thoughts and some were about the company and our progress, but we never had a candidate come to an interview who was not at least familiar with what we do and our progress.

You don't need to be that radical, of course. It is not easy. But be consistent. Try to keep your social networks active, with at least a post or two a week where you discuss new stuff happening, what you're working on, new clients, new education, conferences you were a part of, and media articles you were in.

Try to get your founders onto podcasts, in media articles, and as speakers at relevant conferences where your clients and/or potential candidates attend. Make sure people have heard of you before you need to engage with them!

Some will hate you and make jokes that they are "afraid to open a can of soda because you might pop up there," but that just means you're doing the right thing.

If You Talk the Talk, Walk the Walk

So, now you're on social media, on all startup sites, available everywhere, sharing your progress, everyone has heard of you, and you've built hype. Awesome! But make sure that the hype is not fake. Nothing puts people off more than fake advertising.

If you've said you're working on something or are working with a client, make sure you actually are. Make sure you deliver. All the time, every time. If you build fake hype, people will see through it immediately, and then your startup will not be attractive to anyone.

---

[1] www.linkedin.com/feed/hashtag/?keywords=postadaymm

CHAPTER 8   GUEST CHAPTER: RECRUITING IN A STARTUP ENVIRONMENT

In his book *Influence*, Robert B. Chialdini says that committing to something publicly is a great way of actually making yourself do it. So, the constant feedback loop of saying something on social media, then doing it, then reporting about it is an awesome way to keep pushing yourself and your startup[2].

Recruiting From Personal Channels

We've never put a job opening on one of those job opening sites. We have never needed to. By building up an online presence, we ended up just needing to share the link and people who had already heard of the company and liked it automatically got to see the posts.

From my experience, it is much better to have people who have previously shown interest in you apply for your jobs. Also, people who have heard of you and see your post about a job opening can always suggest their acquaintances. Recommendations from people you already know are always a bonus!

No-Bullshit Job Descriptions

You do need a landing page with your job opening, regardless of whether you are using a job-finding site or not. This landing page needs to describe these few things accurately, briefly, and honestly:

- What the recruiting startup actually is
- What the position is
- What the startup expects from the candidate

---

[2] Robert B. Cialdini, *Influence: The Psychology of Persuasion, Revised Edition* (New York, NY: Harper Business, 2006)

- What can the startup offer the candidate (yes, it's a two-way street!)
- What the interview process is going to be like

Let's briefly discuss these points.

Describe the Startup

Google "how to pitch a startup." There are a few exercises I found useful:

1. Pitch your startup in six words or less.
2. Find three main supporting topics about why your startup is awesome.
3. Describe your traction (clients and revenue only for pitching to investors), awards, and recognition.
4. Describe your market through plans and ambitions.

Now you can make a concise and accurate no-bullshit presentation about your startup. Be honest about the team size, company size, ambitions, and so on. Don't present your startup as being Google if it is not. Present it as what it is, because by doing so you're presenting that you're always straight up with people, and people appreciate that!

Describe the Position

Describe the position with as few buzzwords as possible and in as few generic phrases as possible. Phrases like "working on top-notch tech stacks in a dynamic, ever-growing environment ensured to keep you on your toes" make people (author included) sick to their stomach.

Keep it simple. "We are a startup with an in-house development team of three people and are looking for a front-end developer with skills in Typescript and Angular to join our team."

List Expectations of the Candidate

Be clear about what skills you need the person to have. This is also a good exercise for the startup itself, because by thinking about this they are actually made to think about what problems this new person needs to solve.

Do not ask for things you do not need. Very often you see openings looking for a front-end JavaScript developer with database management skills, or openings for a project manager who is a marketing expert. Doing this will

- Not attract people, because those are skills that don't necessarily go together.
- Attract jacks of all trades who can do all those things ... poorly.
- Attract jacks of all trades who can do all those things well ... but are well above your pay grade.

Describe What the Startup Is Offering the Candidate

The eternal debate is should job opening posts include the salary or not? I vote yes. Even if your salary is less than the market average, the fact you're a cool startup can attract amazing candidates. Sure, people will comment that you offer inadequate conditions and such, but people who have "better conditions" than you are offering but still find time to troll your posts with comments about it are just sad and need help.

My advice is to be honest and open because this is your strongest card when you're a small startup. Be straight up about working hours, equipment, expectations, and company culture. The more you're open about it and share, the more comfortable the candidates will feel about you before even meeting you.

Describe the Interview Process

A timeline:

- Gathering resumes until May 15
- Test task until May 22
- Interviewing until May 29
- Final decision on May 30

And stick to it! This is another place where you can show that you actually deliver on what you say you deliver.

Communication with Candidates

Answer every job application. Always. No exceptions. It is as simple as that.

We did a thing where, if for one reason or another we did not decide on a candidate, we did our best to find similar position openings and share those links with the candidates so they could find a different opportunity. It's a small gesture, but it makes you look nice and will pay off in the future. Or at least it has for my startup.

Communicate clearly, respond fairly quickly, and be clear about the next steps. That is pretty much all the advice I can provide here.

Task Before the Interview

Another thing the Internet debates a lot about is whether it is okay to present candidates with a task. My opinion is

- If they are entry-level for a position, then definitely yes.
- If they are experienced in a position, then ask them to provide some of their previous work for you to take a look at and discuss in the interview.

Candidates who refuse tasks speaks loudly about their attitude, and this is not something I'd like in my company, especially in a startup environment. In a startup environment, you will end up needing to wear many hats and often do things outside your normal job scope, outside of your expertise, and even outside of your comfort zone. I wouldn't want to have someone so quick to say "I won't do that" on my team.

Interview Process

This needs to be as short, simple, and straightforward as possible. Some companies have three to five interviews, intelligence tests, psychological evaluations, and more.

This is all bullshit. You're looking for amazing people. However, if they are indeed amazing, then other companies will be looking at how to get their hands on them, too! So, if you want them to join your startup, don't drag the process out. Otherwise, they might get snatched by others.

The job interview is, unfortunately, a beauty contest. Someone who is not the best fit might be very charming and talkative and get you to hire them. Someone who is a good fit might be scared, confused, or just blocked, and you'll pass up on them. It's just how it goes; there is no way around this. But try your best and trust your gut feeling.

A few tips for the interview process that have worked well for us are:

- Start by telling the candidate what it was about their resume and/or task that you liked and why you called them in. It is nice to show that you actually read their CV, rather than starting with, "Can you tell me the stuff about yourself that I could have read on your CV?"

- Also, present your company briefly. They should have read more before the interview, and if they didn't, they'll have a chance to ask in the end.

- If you ask a question and/or have given a task, don't judge just the solution. Judge the approach, consider the amount of work and effort, and try to evaluate the level of detail and dedication. If a person puts in a lot of effort and shows they are thorough, responsible, and detail-oriented, the fact that they've given a wrong answer might not be relevant. In the end, they will learn the job on the job, and there is no way of getting around that.
- Check if a person is easy to communicate with and if they are flexible. In a dynamic environment such as a startup, these are the two most important qualities (in my opinion).

In the end, pull the trigger. If you like the candidate, hire them. If you don't, be honest about what you didn't like. If you liked everything, but there were better candidates, that is fine, too!

For countries with overly complex legislation, like Croatia, make sure you have the maximum allowed "trial period." The trial period in Croatia means that you work normally and that the salary is normal. However, if it isn't working out, it makes it easy for you to terminate the contract with the reasoning that "the trial period was not satisfactory." Otherwise, you can get into legal complications with how to terminate a contract. This is the fun part of having a startup in a country with too much poorly-written legislation.

Onboarding

Make sure you have the onboarding process ready. There is nothing worse than having a new team member jump aboard and then not knowing what to do with them.

CHAPTER 8   GUEST CHAPTER: RECRUITING IN A STARTUP ENVIRONMENT

Onboarding is important and the things you need to make sure to explain to the new person are

- **What the company is and what you do**: It is very common that people don't really get this from your website or pitches because it might be wrapped in marketing jargon. Be clear, brutally honest, and show inputs and outputs.

- **Explain the company culture**: What are the values that are important and why? How do you uphold them? This is important because it will allow the new person to fit in with the team.

- **Explain the expectations and responsibilities**: Explain clearly when you expect them to work, how to communicate, how to report, who to report to, and what their measurable output should be. You always want your teammates to be absolutely clear on what it is they need to be doing to help the startup in the best possible way.

- **Meet the people**: Introduce the new person to the heads of departments they'll be working with. Explain the company hierarchy if you have one. Explain the meetings and reports that are used between departments.

- **Make sure they understand that you are a startup**: There are processes and procedures, but sometimes shit will hit the fan. Then it is just a matter of doing your best and doing anything you can to help the company. At that point (if it happens, and it will happen) all roles, procedures, and systems go out the window and we all jump in to put the fire out the best way we know how.

Feedback Loop

There should be managers who will monitor the work of the new hire. It is of vital importance that the person gets honest feedback on their work and performance. However, it is also important that the new person has a way of providing feedback of their own. They need to feel comfortable to make suggestions, ask questions, and suggest improvements or alternatives.

In my current company, we set up a monthly one-to-one interview. It's an interview that happens once a month (go figure?) where the manager and the employee can speak to each other completely honestly with no hard feelings, gloves off, as equals. It has helped us identify several problems in time and act accordingly to solve them.

Easy to Hire, Easy to Fire

As we said, being a startup, you don't want to have a hiring process lasting ten weeks and through seven rounds of interviews. You want to hire fast!

Unfortunately, as difficult as it may be, the same thing is required when ending an employment contract. If a person is not living up to the expectations, you need to address it quickly.

Make sure that your employee knows whether they are doing great or poor work. In both cases, make sure you tell them why, what you are proud of, and what they should improve upon.

If they get a few pieces of feedback stating they are not improving the same thing, you need to terminate the contract. This is never easy and never comfortable, and we have prolonged this for months in a few situations, hoping things would solve themselves, but they never do. If it isn't working out and you see it's not on a good path, act now. It will not magically turn itself around. However, do make sure that you have given the other person a chance and a warning telling them it isn't working, why it isn't working, and what they should improve.

If termination needs to be done, be honest and upfront about it. It sucks, and you'll feel bad about it, but you know it's the best thing to do, so just do it. The faster, the better!

In most European countries, especially the southern and eastern ones, it is extremely difficult to fire someone who has been hired full-time. Startups often need to be legally creative to get rid of dead weight or employees who simply don't fit.

Stock Options

Being in Croatia makes things tricky in terms of stock options. Our legislation is so far behind the more developed world that stock options are very tricky and clumsy to do.

However, in the rest of the world, it is customary to offer stock options to your employees. This is, in my opinion, a great thing and will help onboard ambitious people and keep them excited about the project. How much, when, and at what valuation is very individual and I don't know what advice to provide here. So, good luck with finding optimal stock options. If you do, please blog about it, and provide me with a link!

Conclusion

You will hire some amazing people, and you will also make some terrible mistakes when hiring people. Hire people you feel comfortable talking to, communicating with, working with, and giving responsibilities to.

Always, always, treat all your candidates and hires with respect and honesty. You, as an upcoming startup, don't have the best conditions to offer, but respect and honesty are free and often matter the most.

Always make sure you do your best to make the relationship and the engagement work. If it works well, make sure that the person knows what you are happy about and why. And make sure you reward them for their effort. If it doesn't, the same thing applies: make sure they know why and what they can improve.

And if it isn't working out, don't be afraid to pull the plug. You have a responsibility to your business.

PERSONAL EXAMPLE: LEARNING HOW TO FIRE

Hiring is never easy, and firing is often harder. But, postponing the inevitable just increases the consequences of having a bad employee around. It took me too long to realize this the first time it happened, but it was a valuable experience, which guided me to be quick both on hiring and on firing.

CHAPTER 9

Managing Money

> **TL;DR**
>
> - A startup is always out of money...and founders have even less.
> - Buy what you need, quickly!
> - Keep an eye on EBITDA.

The Root of All Evil

If you want to create something, you need money to do it. But once you get the money, what then?

If that money comes from VCs, or really any investors, the answer is definitely not "transfer it to the founders' accounts." Sometimes, there will even be contractual clauses that govern the founders' salaries. The nominal reasons are that the investors want all their money to go into the growth of the company, and that the founders will get a big payout when they exit the company down the line or sell off a portion of their shares, but in reality, there are other factors to it, such as keeping the founders "hungry" so they "perform better."

CHAPTER 9   MANAGING MONEY

That's a bit unlucky for the founders. There are many reports out there[1] that basically state that founders in the pre-seed phase will pay themselves a salary that is maybe 10% to 15% larger than the general *country average* (which for IT or other high-tech workers often comes down to being a very small salary) and wait until about the series A investment to pay themselves a bit more than the *industry average*. There are even "romantic" ideas floating around of imitating high-profile CEOs like Steve Jobs and Elon Musk, who paid themselves $1 salaries.

There is a real and present danger in this kind of thinking, but it is also inevitable. On the one hand, startup companies really need to spend a lot of money to create and market the product, and every penny spent on the founders is a penny not spent to grow the company. On the other hand, as the company gains more investors, the founders lose their equity percentage in the company and can also lose voting power, dividend preferences, or even end up with a type of company stock that gains them nothing after their exit, so if they have just spent a few years starving and now have nothing, they will not be happy.

One typical example[2] is that the founders, as a group, can end up with less than 20% of the company after Series A funding. If the founders were unlucky enough to lose some rights or end up with common stock in a situation where all the investors have preferential stock, that 20% could yield them exactly zero on exit. Imagine that: you work your ass off for five or ten years and have nothing to show for it because you were desperate for that investment. This is not the only example of investors having different goals and priorities than the founders.

---

[1] Such as this one: Sifted, Miriam Partington, "*What do startup founders pay themselves?*" https://sifted.eu/articles/startup-founders-salary/.

[2] From here: Entrepreneur, Stever Robbins, "*Dividing Equity Between Founders and Investors*," www.entrepreneur.com/money-finance/business-dividing-equity-between-founders-and-investors/65028.

CHAPTER 9   MANAGING MONEY

How does the romantic idea of giving yourself no salary or the minimum wage in expectation of a big exit sound now?

You should pay yourself what you are worth.

Time Is Money

One of the qualities of a good founder is recognizing your weak spots and working around them. Sometimes this means hiring other people to do something you can't do or do badly. In an early-stage startup, this can often lead to a situation where you, as a founder, are paying yourself minimum wage but are employing experts who draw an industry average pay (sometimes many times greater than your own).

We all realize that's a bad thing, but sometimes there's nothing you can do about it. Investors will encourage it. The startup community you are a part of will probably laud you for being so self-sacrificing for the success of your startup. But if everything fails (and remember that about 70% of startups fail by the third year, and after a couple of more years, this climbs to about 90%[3]), will you be able to recover?

Even while the startup is operating as usual, if something happens to the founders (maybe they can't pay medical insurance after driving an old beat-up car and crashing, or maybe they fall into depression because their spouse left them for working too hard), the startup will certainly fail. It's like you hear in the pre-flight check on an airplane: if you don't/can't help yourself with an oxygen mask first, you will not be able to help your children.

In business terms, this is closely related to the concept of the *opportunity cost*. If you do this thing (the startup), how much money

---

[3] From Embroker, "*106 Must-Know Startup Statistics for 2023*," www.embroker.com/blog/startup-statistics.

(and other resources, like time) are you losing because you are not doing another thing (like having a career in a corporation)?

A rule of thumb for startups is that they burn money to profit from accelerated development or market presence. If you need to hire experts, buy licenses, tools, or anything that could help you grow, do so as early as possible.

Reinvest Everything

Many VCs will frown upon leaving their money unspent or spent in a way that doesn't directly help the company grow. Ideally, they want the company to always need more money because 1) this means their money is being spent in a way that generates more money in the long term, and 2) because if the company gains traction, they want you to seek more money from them.

Many early-stage startups always hover close to zero in their bank accounts. Not because they want to, but because they have no choice if they want to do the impossible task of having a noticeable market presence with little to no money to spend either on developing the product or on marketing. (If you don't know which to pick between these two, pick spending more money on marketing.)

Once you actually have any kind of noticeable cash flow, you should probably hire a CFO (Chief Financial Officer) to help you plan what to do with it in a way that won't be immediately disastrous for the company. There are people out there who can work as CFOs without being employed full-time (and really, don't need to be for a small company), so seek them out. You'll learn a lot.

The Holy Grail of the EBITDA Margin

Once your company starts to sell something, it will have revenue. Revenue is the total money coming to the company, including the VAT, which will more or less be immediately subtracted. After all expenses and taxes are paid, what remains is net income.

The term "profit" is sometimes used interchangeably with "income," and in companies that deal with software they can be almost the same. Profit is more often used as a temporary measure of a single business deal. For example, the company sells something for a certain gross amount, and there were some expenses involved to create that thing, and the difference between the two is the profit on that transaction.

EBITDA is calculated from the net income, and in startups it usually represents the liquidity of the company, which is how much money it has in its bank accounts for daily expenses, unforeseen expenses, and eventually paying out profits to its investors. EBITDA is a subset of the entire revenue and is calculated by adding some expenses back on top of the net income.

EBITDA = net income + interest on company's debts + company taxes + depreciation + amortization

A software startup will typically not own real estate or a significant amount of machinery (it might own computers and office supplies, for example), so depreciation and amortization will be close to zero.

For early-stage startups, however, net income will also be close to zero. This can be a bad thing when you are trying to raise an investment because in this case EBITDA could also be close to zero, meaning you are struggling to pay even your daily expenses. This is normal to an extent, but if it lasts for more than a couple of years, it might indicate your business is not profitable and thus is uninvestable.

Once your startup has advanced and can show significant income, EBITDA might be used in calculating the company's valuation, by multiplying it with a certain factor that depends on the industry and global economic movements. In well-developed economies, this factor can range from five times for very risky, still-early startups to 15 times for healthy, hockey-stick growing startups to over 30 times for industry darlings and very hyped-up companies.

Unfortunately, when dealing with European VCs, this factor is frequently about 20% less than it should be for the startup to grow significantly from such an investment to compete on the global scale, and in Eastern European countries it can be up to 50% less. Unfortunately, the cost to develop a global product is usually not as low as those percentages presume, since your company is competing on a global level for the same people as the companies that can pay more, and all of Europe is extremely well connected to the richer countries worldwide. Some VCs thus do themselves and your startup a disservice when they cripple the company from further or faster growth.

Because of the use of the EBITDA multiple/factor, it's sometimes said that it's better for a startup not to have any revenue (a pre-revenue startup) than low revenue. You will need to decide on this as a founder.

The EBITDA margin is the ratio between EBITDA and the total revenue. A good, healthy company is expected to have an EBITDA margin of around 10% or more.

In early-stage companies, valuation is usually not done by EBITDA but by analyzing its revenue, revenue sources, and growth. Usually, a certain multiple in the range of five to ten is applied to the revenue to arrive at a type of valuation. As valuation is still a very subjective notion, it is the founders' job to increase it and use the best method of calculating it, but you should be aware that the investors' job is to undervalue your company so they can get more profit from it when you grow.

All of this may or may not be aligned with the theory that says the valuation of the business represents its future earnings.

There's also "adjusted EBITDA" which adds some more elements back to the net profits, mostly one-time expenses, but sometimes also R&D, which could be a significant amount for a startup.

On Growth

If you have investors, they will almost certainly require constant growth from the company, even if you, as founders, do not (in which case you probably want a lifestyle business, not a startup).

Early on, since you are starting from nothing, it's usual to have growth rates of two, five, or ten times year-on-year (YoY). If you are lucky, this fast growth will continue and sprout into a hockey-stick graph, which will make the company extremely attractive to investors.

After a time, this will settle into a more normal and, up to a point, sustainable "scale-up" growth rate which ranges from 20% to 50%, depending on the industry and the global economy. You should welcome growth and, as much as possible, you should prepare for it and the issues it brings—from hiring the right people to getting the right equipment and services to restructuring your sales process, while constantly keeping an eye on the attractiveness of your product to your customers.

Fast growth attracts investors who are into relatively risky businesses. Once your company establishes itself on the market and lasts a few decades, it will start to attract investors who value stability (but not stagnation) rather than fast returns on investment, such as pension funds.

There are several ways in which growth can be defined and tracked. One down-to-earth way, which is very encouraged by grant-givers and governments in Europe, is by counting the number of employees. This is a good metric since at the very least it forces founders to (more or less suddenly) become responsible for the salaries and well-being of others, which tends to drive business activities. The number of employees is also sometimes a hard condition for receiving certain grants, benefits, or even investments. As a rule of thumb, the founders should delegate things to employees as soon as possible[4] because it also reduces the "bus factor" risk (how much the company suffers if any one person in it gets hit by a bus).

Another popular but useless way of tracking growth is "vanity metrics." These are numbers that might look good on paper but do not directly contribute to the revenue. Examples of these metrics are the number of unpaid/trial/pilot users, the number of followers on social media, the number of page views for a web app, and the number of downloads in an app store. It could be said that all of them are indication of activity and will someday lead to revenue, but the usual issue is that the company cannot show a direct correlation. Vanity metrics can mislead founders into believing they have a good product on their hands, when in fact the only thing that eventually determines that is how well the product sells. A metric becomes "actionable" (or non-vanity) when there's a strong correlation between it and the revenue produced by the company.

Usually, while revenue is the ultimate goal, there are intermediate goals that must be attained to reach it. Examples of worthy goals for startups are

- Increasing monthly recurring revenue (MRR)
- Reaching more customers
- Lowering the customer acquisition cost (CAC)
- Lowering the customer churn rate
- Increasing the customer lifetime value (CLV)
- Increasing the website traffic-to-lead ratio
- Increasing the company liquidity

---

[4] I am talking about "real" salaried, full-time, employees here, not contractors and part-time help.

Usually, working just on the MRR, CAC and CLV goals is good enough (and difficult enough) to get a startup from an early stage to a Series A stage.

How you do it depends on the type of your business and is more art than science. One thing in common to all successful startups is that they try *a lot* of ideas, usually simultaneously. One example of that is the recent "unicorn" company from Croatia, Infobip, which at one startup meetup revealed it's doing about 30 simultaneous experiments in sales, such as A/B tests, repackaging and reframing products and services, trying out new customer niches, new payment/subscription models, and more. An early startup probably doesn't have the money to do all that, but it definitely must try as many things as possible.

PERSONAL EXAMPLE #1: A STRUGGLE TO KEEP AFLOAT

The cash-starved startup has become a trope. For most startups, hovering near zero in their bank account is the "normal" state of affairs until the business starts to pick up. For us, we were constantly balancing between getting enough money into team members' hands so they could actually live normally and reinvesting into the company so it could grow. I don't think there was a single point in time when everyone got what they wanted. It was always a compromise. All founders have a certain responsibility to help the company grow, but the CEO feels it most of all. Decisions of whether to pay team members more or to help the company with those funds are never easy. Retrospectively, I'm glad I've mostly put people's interest first, before the interests of the company, but I'm acutely aware that has slowed down growth a bit.

CHAPTER 9   MANAGING MONEY

PERSONAL EXAMPLE #2: GROWTH AS AN INVESTMENT CRITERION

I used to think growth was the single most important thing that made a company desirable as an investment, but the reality is that it solely depends on the investor. One sobering event was when I returned for the nth time to pitch to a particular VC, who originally suggested we didn't grow enough to be interesting to them. Every time we grew our revenue significantly, I followed up with them and go the same response: grow some more. Finally I was really proud of our latest business deals and hoped they would find us acceptable, but they said they disliked us based on another criterion. It's likely they were never interested in us at all, and nothing happened from my communication with that VC.

CHAPTER 10

Get Your Product Out There

TL;DR

- Your goal is to acquire the largest chunk of your target market in the shortest possible period of time.
- You should anticipate unethical behavior from your competition.
- Create a community of 1,000 true fans of your product and have them enthusiastically recommend it to their friends.

Business Development

There's this term or idea of "business development" (BD), which is defined as "the activity of pursuing strategic opportunities for a particular business or organization, for example by cultivating partnerships or other commercial relationships, or identifying new markets for its products or services." However you want to define it, you need it.

Unfortunately, it is usually very hard and expensive to acquire someone who does *good* business development. In many cases, if no current cofounders can fit this role, you should probably invest extraordinary effort to find someone who can and include them in the founding team, as otherwise you are probably looking at having a very expensive first employee. I know a startup where the founders had to pay 5x their own salary to a high-quality BD employee (it was a successful arrangement, though).

The hugely important qualification here is that the above text refers to a "good" business development person. There is an abundance of people who claim they can do it, and can do it cheaply, but who almost inevitably turn out not to be able to deliver on this promise. A good BD person should be able to:

- Show direct experience addressing your target market (you can't afford to have people learning on the job yet).

- For B2B, be able to form a direct plan to address a dozen or so potential first clients who are NOT their buddies

- Create a sales funnel (or a couple of them) for your product and give an estimation of time and volume of clients moving through each stage

- Create a high-level strategy for your marketing campaigns and oversee its implementation

At the early stages, you probably cannot afford to have separate employees for BD, marketing, and sales. At the very earliest stages, as with all company activities, this is role that will be filled by the founding team.

A good BD person for a **B2B** product is usually outgoing, reasonably extroverted, easy to talk to, and creative in forming deals. They will need to talk to a lot of procurement managers, office heads, other CEOs, and similar people to establish relationships and make business deals. On the other hand, a good **B2C** BD person should probably be more analytical and capable of forming "spray and pray" strategies to reach a huge volume of potential clients on ad platforms and constructing iron-clad sales funnels that have tentacles throughout your product and your company. A B2C strategy for a modern startup is necessarily global and addresses a wide slice of the population. A person who is a great car salesman is not fit for that role. Rather, it's the person who enjoys tweaking SEO knobs.

Pricing Strategies

It might be tempting to underprice your product because you are new on the market. That is usually not the best strategy, since you risk training your potential customers to under-value your product. A better way to do it is to offer discounts and seasonal sales offers.

Other than that, pricing is mostly a consequence of how you position your product in the market. Is it a premium product offered to the upper market segment? Is it the best performing product, allowing customers to do things better than any other product on the market? Or is it a "value" product, offering most common features at an unbeatable price? What other products do you want your customers to compare your product to when they are deciding whether to buy it?

You must decide on the product's positioning before starting to offer it on the market. You might change your mind later, but in any case, you must avoid sending conflicting messages to your prospective clients. Stay with one positioning strategy at a time. If you start promoting your product as a "value" product, it will be very hard to reposition it as "premium" and vice-versa, mostly because people unconsciously form and hold opinions about product positioning which are hard to change. For example, look at Mazda, the car manufacturer. They started by producing affordable cars and kept that image for more than 50 years. For the last 10 years, they have been trying to switch to a premium/upscale market and are facing

CHAPTER 10   GET YOUR PRODUCT OUT THERE

significant difficulties. Customers who got used to buying cheap Mazdas can no longer afford the current models, and premium customers don't (yet) see enough "brand value" in the Mazda name (in terms of bragging rights within their peer group) to consider them worth buying.

Try to avoid being in that kind of situation.

Here are some ways of earning €1 million dollars in revenue:

- Get 100,000 people to pay €10 for your product.
- Get 10,000 people to pay €100 for your product.
- Get 5,000 people to pay €200 for your product.
- Get 1,000 people to pay €1000 for your product.
- Get 500 people to pay €2,000 for your product.
- Get 100 people to pay €10,000 for your product.
- Get 10 people to pay €100,000 for your product.

Where does your product fit? How many people can you reach and in what time? If you are creating a subscription service, here is the same list in terms of monthly payments; the goal again is to reach €1 million a year:

- Get 30,000 people to pay €3/month (€36 yearly).
- Get 10,000 people to pay €9/month (€108 yearly).
- Get 5,000 people to pay €17/month (€204 yearly).
- Get 2,000 people to pay €42/month (€504 yearly).
- Get 1,000 people to pay €83/month (€996 yearly).
- Get 300 people to pay €278/month (€3,336 yearly).

Goals like this can seem both easy and hard. How fast can you acquire 1,000 true fans to pay you €83/month? Or a one-time payment of €1000?

Keep in mind that in the real world, there are transaction fees and taxes, which means that without exception, your bottom line will look much worse if you have 30,000 people paying €3/month than if you have 5,000 people paying €17/month. On the other hand, it's much easier going from 30,000 customers to 100,000 customers than from 5,000 to 18,000.

Selling B2B vs. Selling B2C

B2B and B2C are fundamentally different in many aspects:

B2B	B2C
Addresses a smaller number of clients/businesses that can be helped by the new product, usually up to hundreds in the first couple of years of a startup	Addresses a much wider set of clients/individual consumers who might need or want the product, usually up to millions in the first couple of years of a startup
Issues a couple of big invoices per month	Issues thousands of small invoices daily
It can be harder to turn into a recurring/repeating business relationship.	It's usually easier to extract a small-sum subscription from consumers.
(If not a SaaS product) Has a small-ish team of highly skilled salesmen establishing individual relationships with other companies	Has a couple of digital marketing strategists and large, but usually not as skilled, teams doing customer support and direct sales (if applicable)

It is worth thinking about the strategy you will employ in selling your product. For example, it is ineffective selling a B2C product to individual customers one by one, because the per-customer lifetime revenue will usually be much lower than the investment you need to make for this type of process. It is also usually ineffective for your early stage startup to start selling to businesses by treating them as undifferentiated anonymous users. A much better response will usually be received by treating each B2B client as special and communicating with them a lot.

One thing is usually true in general, regardless of the type of your business: the more expensive the product you are selling, the more personal relationships you need to form with your customers (and remember from earlier chapters: in B2B, your customers are usually not your users). The reason for this is risk mitigation through trust.

Growth Hacking

Growth hacking used to be a hot topic, until it became just another normal business practice. The downside to that is that the competition is stiffer since everyone tries similar techniques to sell their products. In itself, growth hacking tries to find ways of selling products that result in rapid growth of a company, often through engaging customers in unorthodox ways.

One key aspect of growth hacking is that it is a framework for testing out a large number of approaches, picking and adapting as you go. As a startup, your best bet is to grow through activities that are cheap for you to implement but have a high potential of going viral. You will do a lot of A/B testing of your product's features, UX, its branding, and its marketing materials. It's not unusual to have several variations of landing pages, slogans, video clips, and so on for testing different audiences until you find one which "clicks" and attracts the most users.

Again, selling the product often begins with the product itself. Testing growth hacking approaches will usually reveal how making tweaks in the way your product works or how it looks will influence sales. It's very important in the early days to think of product development and sales as parts of a single process that influence each other. You might have the luxury of having completely separate marketing and sales departments later on, but for now, you need to find out what works to find your first *product-market fit*.

Some growth hacking approaches worth trying are

- (For B2B) Send highly personalized introductory messages (through e-mail, LinkedIn, or even snail-mail) offering to help your potential business partner with your product.

- Offer a free trial or a freemium version of your product because there is a huge mental barrier between using a "free" product and paying even €1 for it.

- Implement referral or affiliate marketing by offering your users rewards if they recommend your product, possibly within your product UX (e.g., offer free subscriptions/points/feature tiers to users who onboard their friends).

- Create educational content (blogs, YouTube videos) for the industry sector your product is in, subtly (it must be subtle, or it will get boring fast!) referencing your own product.

- Build a community around your product or brand on a single platform of your choosing. Find your "1,000 true fans" who will also be your evangelists and attract new customers[1].

---

[1] A very useful concept. Read about it at Technium, "1000 True Fans," https://kk.org/thetechnium/1000-true-fans/

- Think in terms of sales funnels, not individual sales. If you can get a person to leave their e-mail address in exchange for an e-book you've written about the problem you are solving (only indirectly mentioning your product), you know they are interested in your product and can send them low-intensity e-mails for years in the future until they convert to as customer.

- (Mostly for B2B) Create webinars and live lecture sessions which solve a particular problem to attract interest to your brand and your product.

- (For B2C) Create crowdfunding campaigns even if you don't need them or fit the crowdfunding model since it's still a way to reach a wide audience of people who are interested in what you are doing.

- Try to be constantly present in media relevant to your industry, such as forums, Discords, subreddits, Twitch channels, and YouTube comments. It improves your chances of being noticed or even recognized as a thought leader in the industry.

There are, of course, many other strategies worth exploring. Since this area is rapidly changing all the time, I won't reference a book here. Instead, I encourage you to explore and search for ideas on these topics online. What worked 5 or 10 years ago might not work today.

Survival of the Most Tenacious

You will probably find that getting your startup on the market is putting you in the most competitive environment you have ever faced. It's brutal out there. If you've heard about Type A and Type B personalities, entrepreneurship, and startups in particular, are where Type A personalities thrive. This is not to say that you in particular need to be a ruthlessly organized workaholic, but even so, a lot of your competition will be.

The free market is often very Darwinian in nature. It's where people and ideas are constantly facing competition and are evaluated for their "fitness," and where extinction of companies is a natural event. The only problem is that "fitness" conditions are always changing and are usually unpredictable. A good idea is often a good idea only within a specific time window, and if you, your team, and your company are not ready, the opportunity will slip away. Even if you are ready and bring a product to the market when the market needs it, you can be absolutely certain that those needs will soon shift, and you should build a company that shifts with them.

It's not only "the market" (as in consumers and customers) that influences your success. Your competition will also do whatever it can to succeed, even if it involves directly harming your company in unethical or even illegal ways. Here are some examples of "dark" practices I have personally come across where the competition was rough:

- **Copycats:** You really do not need to be worried about anyone copying your product (or ideas in general) in the early stage. No one is crazy to spend resources copying an unproven product. But as soon as you achieve success, meaning when your business model is validated and you start gaining customers and nontrivial revenue, there will be copycats, especially if you are in the software business. This is why it is important for a company to protect its IP in the early stage, while they are still not interesting enough to be copied. A very interesting subtype of copycats are unscrupulous VCs whose business model is to create direct copies of semi-successful products, going after the exact same markets, with the goal that their copy is bought (only to be closed off/destroyed) by VCs backing the original startup, to preserve their original investment. You can only fight them off by having a faster time to market, by taking a huge market share early, or by having enough money to beat them in the game.

- **Paying for bad reviews:** This one is so common it's no longer an outlier. You can be almost certain that your competitors will buy fake bad customer reviews of your products on whatever marketplaces or review sites they appear. There are services out there where bad actors can buy bad reviews in bulk, thousands of them, which can range from simply leaving a low number of stars to leaving bad review comments. Your only defense is to be vigilant and notice when it happens and then try to communicate to the platform in question to take down the reviews.

- **Paying for good reviews:** Similar to the previous case, but sometimes your competitors pay for *positive fake reviews* on your product, in a way that is really obvious to the platform owners. The goal here is to make the platform owners think *you* are buying the fake reviews, leading them to censor or even kick your product off the platform for breaching their terms of service. This is harder to fight against and really depends on the good relationship between you and the platform's customer service.

- **Paying for misleading ads:** This has become a standard business practice in the last decade or so[2]. Competitors will buy ads on search-related platforms and services for words and phrases related to your product, but the ad clicks will lead to *their* product instead. Their ads sometimes have creative and compelling wording and can completely cut your startup off from a particular advertising medium. Unfortunately, it's really hard to fight this one off without having the money to outspend the competition.

- **Draining your marketing funds with fraudulent clicks:** This is also called *click fraud* and is done by bots clicking on your ads on different platforms, wasting your ad budget and providing no benefits to your company. Click fraud is also very hard to fight off without outspending your competition. The last two cases are not adequately handled by the ad companies since those kinds of bidding wars benefit them financially.

- **Falsely reporting your product**: Similarly to paying for good or bad fake reviews, unscrupulous competitors might buy a bot service that reports your product on various platforms, including app stores, ad platforms, and social media platforms, accusing the product of breaching various terms of service. In many cases, it can lead to the product being banned from the platforms in question. This type of attack can *usually* be

---

[2] The Guardian, "*Scammers Can Create Fake Business Ads in Google Within Hours,*" www.theguardian.com/money/2020/jul/06/scammers-can-create-fake-business-ads-on-google-within-hours

resolved by contacting the platforms' customer service desks, but it can be devastating if it happens on the day you are launching an important new update or a feature.

This list is yet another reason why founding a startup is better described as a "calling" than as a "job."

This list also illustrates the importance of quickly reaching a substantial chunk of your target market: aside from having money to outspend them, this is your best bet at defending against unethical practices from your competition.

Use ChatGPT and Other Content Generators Where You Can

Since you are addressing a global audience, and very likely cannot get native English speaking members on your team, you should be getting very friendly with ChatGPT and any other tools you can get your hands on that can help you create content and marketing materials.

But don't just copy-paste the generated content into your landing pages or LinkedIn posts. Some actual intelligence is still needed.

Here are six hands-on ideas how you can benefit from generative AI:

- Use ChatGPT to translate your text into proper English by literally asking it to "translate the following text to English."

- Use ChatGPT to fill in the details of client personas by writing prompts like "what would a person liking video games also like?" and "what do Europeans aged 20 to 25 years old spend money on?"

- Use ChatGPT to generate snippets of blog posts and marketing material with prompts like "write a romantic advertising post about a dating site for cat lovers and dog haters" and "write an exciting announcement about a new feature of the SaaS product "Cat Lovers Galore" which makes it easier and much quicker to find dog lovers" Go through the generated text carefully to correct any factual errors and to remove repetitive phrases.

- Use Midjourney to generate images of your client personas to help you better visualize them when putting together marketing strategies, with prompts like "businesswoman, well educated, determined but gentle, forward looking, affluent, living in a middle-class urban setting, with a spacious house, who loves cats and keeps them as pets."

- Use Midjourney to generate your brand's mascot, a virtual avatar that will represent it in virtual chatrooms, metaverses, and other up-and-coming interfaces, with prompts like "a colorful drawing in anime style of Quoraa, a teenage girl full of bubbly optimism, always discovering new ways of having fun, dressed in trendy but not too expensive clothes which sit loosely on her frame, with an unruly red hair and round glasses. She makes friends easily and is teaching them about cool new apps." After a few iterations of these, you could give the result to an actual artist or a 3D modeler to get the final result.

- Use ChatGPT to generate more elaborate prompts for Midjourney.

CHAPTER 10   GET YOUR PRODUCT OUT THERE

Ideally, you would only use these results as starting points or templates for generating actual results.

PERSONAL EXAMPLE: WHEN TO START BUSINESS DEVELOPMENT

It took a long time for me to realize that good business development can be done even for an imperfect product. During the early stages, the founding team was very strained because we thought the product must have such-and-such features before "real" business development could start—and so it got delayed ever more. What we should have done instead is experiment with business development and let BD influence how the product is built. Thinking about it in retrospect, it's obvious that it should be this way, but it took some time to apply in practice.

CHAPTER 11

The Big Exit Theory

> **TL;DR**
>
> - Your company might have a different destiny than you yourself.
> - If aiming for business longevity, be ready to embrace change.
> - If building for an exit, it helps a lot if you do it deliberately.

Keep Your Head On

Startups are difficult. They are about making something a lot of people want and bringing it to them, despite the huge number of obstacles in the way, including simply how to reach those people because their attention is constantly being pulled in different directions.

A lot of people have found comfort in reading *Meditations* by Marcus Aurelius[1], and I count myself among them. It's kind of comforting to read that the Roman emperor had nearly the same problems 2000 years ago as we are experiencing in modern society. Besides, building a successful startup is not that much different from building an empire.

---

[1] Marcus Aurelius, *Meditations* (New York, NY: Penguin, 2005).

© Ivan Voras 2023
I. Voras, *The European VC-Funded Startup Guide*,
https://doi.org/10.1007/978-1-4842-9520-5_11

CHAPTER 11   THE BIG EXIT THEORY

You will face mountains of problems. You will probably want to quit on at least a quarterly basis. You will need to juggle and rearrange resources (and that includes people) in a way you never thought possible, all in order to make things work out smoothly. They often will not.

Doing all this in Europe just adds to the effort because you will almost certainly feel that the society and its laws are actively trying to stop you growing, in many cases because of the strong socialist heritage. The more to the south you are, the worse it gets. You are not alone in this. Find yourself a "tribe" of cofounders and when you stop commiserating with each other, you will probably find at least some workarounds and advice from people on the same path as you.

If you can apply a touch of detachment and find the certainty in yourself that, even if everything fails, you will almost certainly succeed again from scratch, it might give you comfort and a reason to treat yourself as a decent human being. Do that.

What If You Succeed?

Again, running a startup is one of the hardest things in the world to do, and this doesn't really change whether the startup is eventually a success or if it fails. Unfortunately, statistics like those from Embroker[2] show that 90% of all startups fail, regardless of industry. Of those, 10% fail in the first year and about 70% do not survive their fifth year. Looking at it from the optimistic side, if your business survives for five years, there's a good chance it will continue to exist and be reasonably successful.

In previous chapters, I have mostly assumed one possible path for a successful company: it continues to exist and grow for decades, acquiring customers, growing its market share, and eventually becomes a stable

---

[2] Embroker, "106 Must-Know Startup Statistics for 2023," www.embroker.com/blog/startup-statistics/

"blue chip" company, transforming itself often to adapt to new market trends. The ability to adapt is the single most important feature of long-lived companies. It doesn't mean the company needs to switch industries on a whim, but what it does need to do is occasionally change the way it is doing business in accordance with market changes. Take IBM, for example, the oldest surviving IT company, founded in a time before computers as we know them today (1911). There was a time where it was the single biggest IT company in the world, producing hardware and software on an unprecedented scale. It was rarely alone in an industry; it had healthy competition on all sides, but it simply outlasted most of them. To illustrate my point, here are some cherry-picked things IBM did in its 112-year history (as of 2023):

- Switched from producing mechanical (yes, clockwork, cogs-and-wheels!) employee time-keeping systems, punched card equipment, automated meat slicers, and weighing scales to producing electrical computers

- Switched from producing business-only room-sized computers which required scientists to operate to making personal computers, creating the PC in the process and kicking off an era where everyone has one

- Stopped relying on PCs and large business computer systems ("big iron") and started producing laptops as the first portable devices, kicking off an era of mobile computing

- Gave up most of its hardware production to switch to software services, business orchestration, and a consultancy business

These are huge changes. It takes courage and well-developed internal procedures to make the decision to steer the huge company (almost 300,000 employees) in a different direction. Even so, it made some obvious

CHAPTER 11   THE BIG EXIT THEORY

(in retrospect, of course) mistakes, such as not recognizing the potential of the Internet and not embracing cutting edge technologies in a way which would enable them to acquire small companies as clients to grow with them (again related to the Internet, as that's where new clients are). Today, it mostly coasts on its existing big clients, and if it doesn't do something similarly radical as 90 years ago, it may well stop existing in a couple of years. Chances are that it will change successfully simply because it did so before and the company has that kind of experience in its structure.

The key to company longevity is its ability to change and adapt to whatever the market wants. You don't want to be stuck in IBM's "we do clockwork mechanisms" phase forever.

Building for an Exit

There are many reasons why the founders might want to exit the company they've created, ranging from wanting the money to start something new to personal medical issues. Creating a company for the explicit purpose of selling it to a bigger company has become a legitimate business model in the 21st century.

If you are building for an exit, you probably want to keep the following strategic questions on your mind (and on a post-it note on your monitor):

- **Why would a company buy/merge with your company?** Is it to acquire your customers? Your developers (so-called *acqui-hire*)? Your IP? Is it to shut your company down because it's getting in their way? It is usually just one of these and it's not worth your effort to build your strategy in multiple directions.

- **Which type of company is most likely to buy yours?** If explicitly building your company to sell it later, it's very desirable to have a ready list of companies that are your main "targets."

- **When will you reach desirability?** In other words, which conditions need to be fulfilled before your company is likely to get bought. If you are a deep tech company, it's probably when you develop the tech and demonstrate it in practice. If you are a B2C platform, it's probably when you acquire millions of users.

- **What will be your future role?** Will you agree to lead your team as a division of the new company? Usually, the acquiring company will want to keep you because it reduces the risk of the team falling apart (unless they did it for the IP or to get your company off the market).

In any case, cultivate a relationship with your prospective buyers. If they have a presence at industry conferences and other events, you should be there presenting your company. Meet their CEOs and managers; try to make friends there. Keep them informally in the loop about the progress you are making with your company. If you hear rumours that they are considering acquisitions, remind them that your option exists, even explicitly.

As with everything, there's a possibility this strategy will fail. Probably the most devastating failure mode is if the company you've hoped would buy your startup simply skips you and buys another company with similar features. In that case, you might end up with a company that can only grow with the resources you (currently) don't have (but would have had within the bigger company), or even worse, with a company you personally don't want to lead past its current stage. Both are legit outcomes. It pays more to be an optimist, but you should at least have the beginnings of a plan in case that happens.

CHAPTER 11   THE BIG EXIT THEORY

Define "Win"

While miracles sometimes do happen and the good guys win (e.g. those with the best product), it's far more common that the winners are those who are most obstinate, stubborn, and gritty.

Fortunately, this might depend on how you define "winning." Many companies started out with the goal of conquering the world (and I suggest you don't found a startup if you don't have this as a goal, because it will help you endure the process), but have later discovered they objectively can't. By far the two most common reasons for that are very simple: either they don't have the right team to do it, including founders themselves, or the addressable market is too small. As your startup grows, you will need to acquire employees who will launch it into the next phase, and with each phase of growth, there are fewer and fewer people in the world who have experience with that kind of a task. This is especially hazardous if you are headquartered in a region of the world where there are no companies of similar type and scale, in which case you are very limited in your opportunities to find advisors and mentors who have been in your shoes. On the other hand, you might have the right people, but there's simply no interest in what you are producing, and for some reason you can't pivot to something else (maybe the people you have are only good for the current product). In any case, it might become obvious that the company is not growing like it's supposed to and the founders need to decide what's next.

The optimal path for your mental health is to decide that the point you've reached is a "win," whatever it might be. You've started with way less knowledge, contacts, and ideas and you have grown significantly. You can be a mentor to others. Your company will probably continue to exist, and maybe you want to keep it existing while you go do something else. With a good top management team, it might even exist for decades and be one of the pillars of the industry, maintaining a more-or-less steady chunk of the market.

Another path is to become even more obstinate, stubborn, and gritty, and find the strength for yet another push, yet another effort at getting to the top, conquering the peak, to prove to yourself that you can. There's nothing wrong with this approach either, as long as you are enjoying what you are doing. If it becomes a chore, if you find yourself dreading waking up in the morning to go to fight another day, you should definitely stop and re-evaluate your decisions, unless you think PTSP is fun.

PERSONAL EXAMPLE: DO WE NEED TO BUILD FOR AN EXIT?

I received advice at one time that, *it's useless to compete in the global market by ourselves, that we should create a product whose only purpose was to get acquired by a big company instead*. That basically boiled down to, *don't create what you want – create what the big company wants*.

This could be a legit strategy but I felt it would stiffly my, and the team's, creativity. On the other hand, we might have exited by now if we did that. Who knows.

CHAPTER 12

Find Your Replacement(s)

This is a short one.

As a founder, stop doing what you were doing in the earliest stages of your company as soon as possible. You were probably burdened with everything from developing the product, to managing (and cleaning) the office, to finding early clients, to managing marketing.

Your duties in the next phases will likely be completely different. It will still be your company, but now it needs something else from you: more abstract thinking, more networking, more focusing on *what* the business will be instead of *how* the business will operate. More and more you will find yourself doing strategic decision-making and less and less doing the low-level operative stuff. If you don't, your company will not grow. This is when you absolutely need to stop working on the product and start working on the business.

Ideally, empower and educate people from within to become managers. This is the quickest route and is less resource-intensive than introducing managers from outside the company. Be wary of MBAs until you become a huge corporation, because they are not ready for the insanity of the startup environment.

CHAPTER 12 FIND YOUR REPLACEMENT(S)

Pick people based on their passion.

A good book to read at this point is *Anything You Want* by Derek Sivers[1].

Good luck!

---

[1] Sivers, *Anything You Want,* 3rd Edition (Hit Media, 2022)

Index

A

Agencies startups, 29
    approaches, 37
    blue ocean market, 30
    creative person, 31, 32
    European startups, 41
    hedging, 40
    investors, 35
    lifecycle, 38, 39
    liquidity, 36
    potential success, 34, 35
    recurring revenue, 32–34
    scaling, 32
    solvent business, 36
    startups, 36
    staying afloat, 36
    stealth-mode startup, 30, 31
    uncultured, 37

B

Business development (BD)
    B2B and B2C, 141, 142
    ChatGPT, 148–150
    click fraud, 147
    copycats, 145
    definition, 137, 150
    generative AI, 148
    growth hacking, 142–144
    hacking approaches, 143
    marketing/sales, 138
    personalities thrive, 145–149
    positive fake reviews, 146
    pricing strategies, 139–141
    product-market fit, 143
    qualification, 138
    spray/pray strategies, 139

C

Cofounders, *see* Founders time
Convertible loan agreements/notes (CLN), 26, 27
Croatian startup community, *see* Legal section
Customer acquisition cost (CAC), 134, 135
Customer lifetime value (CLV), 134, 135

D

Dioničko društvo (DD), 23
društvo sa ograničenom odgovornošću (DOO), 23
Due diligence (DD) process, 87

E

Employee Share Purchase Plan (ESPP), 109
Employee Stock Ownership Plan (ESOP), 89, 109–111
European (EU) startup
    agencies startups, 41
    benefits, 2
    bootstrapped startups, 5–7
    capability, 12
    concept, 1
    contradictory things, 7
    corporation, 15–17
    gaps (gradients), 11–13
    global business, 7–11
    governmental funds, 62, 63
    key benefits, 6
    marketing agencies, 17
    metaphor, 3
    productive, 3
    Rammstein, 3
    scaling mindset, 4
    service businesses, 13
    startup environment, 159
    types, 14, 15

F, G, H, I, J, K

Founders time
    communication, 103
    definition, 102
    divorce/depression/addictive disorders, 102
    Employee Stock Ownership Plan, 109–111
    Equinox Vision, 111
    iterations, 103
    money, 127
    option pool, 108, 109
    personal skills, 105, 106
    red flag, 103
    remote working, 106
    rules, 107, 108
    tax timing, 110
    technical expertise, 105
    vesting, 109
Franchise business model
    benefits, 45
    business partners/territory, 50
    concepts, 44, 45
    conventional wisdom, 47
    definition, 44
    entrepreneurs, 48
    expert working process, 48, 49
    fees summary, 52–56
    investors/potential buyers, 53
        characteristics, 54
        internal processes, 56
        productivity, 55
        scalability, 55
        time spent development, 55
    mega corporations, 44
    network/market knowledge, 46
    profitable/scalable, 47
    profit generation streams, 50–52
    reasons, 46

INDEX

selling factor, 47
startups, 56, 57

L
Legal section, 20
    articles of association (AOA), 27
    company incorporation, 22, 23
    entity, 23–25
    investments, 25–28
    Paušalni obrt, 25
    relationship, 21
    shareholder agreement (SA), 27
    sharing/protecting ideas, 20
Lifestyle business, 30, 31
Limited liability companies (LLCs), 15, 16, 23, 88, 108, 111

M, N, O, P, Q, R
Money
    capitalization table, 59
    cash-starved startup, 135
    company shares, 87–89
    contractual clauses, 127
    convertible loans, 61
    dilution, 87
    due diligence (DD) process, 87
    EBITDA margin, 131, 132
    equity/cap table, 59
    EU/governmental funds, 62, 63
    expectation, 129
    financial lifecycle, 80–84
    founders, 89
    friends, fools, and family phase, 74
    funding projects, 62
    grants, 60
    growth requirements, 133–135
    investment, 136
    investment contract rules, 85
    investors
        environments, 70
        functional fridge, 66
        honeymoon phase, 64
        incubators/accelerators, 68
        investment progress, 82
        landing page, 64–66
        MVP stage, 66
        pension funds and ETFs, 69
        potential investors, 73
        red flags, 75, 76
        requirements, 65
        sensibilities, 69
        strategic partners, 69
        types, 66–69
        value investors, 75
        VC funds, 68
    pre-money valuation, 90
    product, 60, 61
    product improvements, 75
    reinvest, 130
    requirements, 85
    rules, 84–86
    runway startups, 77–80
    smart money, 71
    spend production, 76
    time, 129, 130

INDEX

Money (*cont.*)
  tracking growth, 134
  trademark, 90
  VC funds, 71–74
monthly recurring revenue (MRR), 134

S

Software-as-a-Service, 13
Startup environment, 151
  exit building process, 154, 155
  history, 153
  no-bullshit job descriptions
    communication, 119
    descriptions, 117
    feedback loop, 123
    hiring process, 123
    Internet debates, 119
    interview process, 119, 120
    job opening posts, 118
    landing page, 116
    list expectations, 118
    onboarding, 122
    position phrases, 117
    stock options, 124
  optimal path, 156
  personal channels, 116
  recruiting process, 114, 115
  socialist heritage, 152
  statistics, 152
  successful company, 152–154
  win definition, 156, 157
  working process, 115, *See also* European (EU) startup

T, U

Term sheet, 98, 99

V, W, X, Y, Z

Valuation process, 94
  definition, 96
  liquidation preference, 99
  network connections, 95
  pre-money/post-money, 97
  subsequent investment, 99
  term sheet, 97–99
  VC money, 95
  vulture/venture capitalists, 94
  5W rule, 94

GPSR Compliance

The European Union's (EU) General Product Safety Regulation (GPSR) is a set of rules that requires consumer products to be safe and our obligations to ensure this.

If you have any concerns about our products, you can contact us on

ProductSafety@springernature.com

In case Publisher is established outside the EU, the EU authorized representative is:

Springer Nature Customer Service Center GmbH
Europaplatz 3
69115 Heidelberg, Germany

www.ingramcontent.com/pod-product-compliance
Lightning Source LLC
LaVergne TN
LVHW010342260326
834688LV00036B/828